Freedom To Succeed

David Kauffman

First Edition: December 2016

Printed in the United States of America

ISBN: 978-1-939237-46-0

Published by Suncoast Digital Press, Inc.

Sarasota, Florida, USA

DEDICATION

This book is dedicated to all the business owners who have struggled for years to make their dream of truly "owning their business" instead of being "owned by their business" ...the ones who stayed up late and got to work early... the ones who found a way to make payroll when it seemed like it couldn't be met... the ones who rolled up their sleeves to get the job done when their best employee quit... the ones who pulled that next customer out of thin air after a sleepless night of uncertainty... the hard-working, determined dreamer...this book is dedicated to you!

PRAISE FOR DAVE KAUFFMAN
AND *FREEDOM TO SUCCEED*

"David Kauffman nails it in *Freedom to Succeed*. The mindset and systems laid out in this book are what every entrepreneur and business owner needs in order to create a sustainable, turnkey business that gives freedom and the ability to succeed…after all, isn't that why we start businesses? You will enjoy and grow from this book."

> —Rod Khleif, Author of *The New Rules of Real Estate, How to Create Lifetime Cash Flow Through Multifamily Properties* and host of the number-one-ranked real estate and business podcast on itunes, "Lifetime Cash Flow through Real Estate Investing."

"*Freedom To Succeed* is a roadmap we can follow for how we can use our memorable life experiences (even from childhood) as fuel for our current passion. It encourages us to dig deep and look for the pearls of value from your earlier years and experience, and how those experiences can serve powerfully as jet fuel to fulfill your current goals and desires…and helps you to leverage what you have learned from the people in your life who you look up to for inspiration.

Dave Kauffman uses personal stories, everything he has learned from his mentors, and experiences gained from working with real people in real-world business situations to help readers achieve freedom…starting today!

> —Lorraine Charles-Hosten, CEO of PharmPro LLC

"*Freedom to Succeed* by David Kauffman is proof positive that we are all capable of greatness. It matters not where you came from, what your background is, or if you are highly educated. What does matter is how passionate and how motivated you are about making your dreams come true. David is a perfect example of that.

The book is filled with proven and practical information, demonstrating what it takes to bring your dreams and desires to fruition. It is well-written with clarity and purpose to give YOU the Freedom to Succeed. Kudos, David, for a job well done.

—Ron Klein, THE GRANDFATHER OF POSSIBILITIES™

Business Consultant, Strategic Advisor, Mentor, Speaker and Inventor of multiple innovations including the magnetic strip on credit and identification cards

"I've had the luxury to work side by side with Dave Kauffman and he is truly a one-of-a-kind, amazing individual. I admire Dave as a radio host, business coach, Godly mouthpiece, and as an incredibly fair, honest human being… and now an author of wisdom and success. Dave Kauffman truly wants the most for others and is committed in action and now in written word, *Freedom To Succeed*. This book will separate you from the 'want to do' and lift you to fulfillment.

Dave Kauffman has helped me immensely, and I'm very grateful. Please read this and realize the freedom of success !!!!"

—Todd Saylor, CEO/President of PayServ Systems

"Dave has 'hit it out of the park' with his new book *Freedom To Succeed*! His years of coaching and speaking to thousands of entrepreneurs have prepared him as a thought leader with real life advice that works. The knowledge you need to *Succeed* is contained in this precious text.

Like Dave, I've spent a lifetime studying successful people and businesses. I know the real deal when I come across it. I have had the honor of learning from Dave, and I'm blessed to call him a mentor. This book is a must for every entrepreneur and business owner!"

—Dr. Ron Eccles, Going Vertical Coaching

CONTENTS

ACKNOWLEDGMENTS ix

FOREWORD xi

INTRODUCTION

The Last of the Free Range Children 1

Chapter 1 - The Diamond Mindset 9

Chapter 2 - "The Cat and Milk Bowl" and Other Highly
Effective Marketing Secrets 13

Chapter 3 - The Systems Will Set You Free 27

Chapter 4 - Sales, the 110% Rule, and Dealing with "D" 43

Chapter 5 - Numbers Don't Lie...But Do They Fly? . . .61

Chapter 6 - The Three "I's" of Leadership 73

Chapter 7 - Projecting Your Worth. 83

Chapter 8 - Sweet Dreams are Made of Goals. 91

Chapter 9 - Next Steps. 115

RESOURCES AND HELPFUL LINKS. 119

ABOUT THE AUTHOR. 120

APPENDIX I - THE BUSINESS DIAMOND
ASSESSMENT™ 123

ACKNOWLEDGMENTS

This book is a result of many people: some good friends, some mentors, some coaches, family...

I would like to acknowledge a few.

First of all, Toni, my beautiful bride—thank you for believing in this project and for your support and love. I could not have the influence I have if it weren't for you!

My father, for teaching me what entrepreneurship looks like, and helping me to not create a comfort zone. Thanks Dad...

Howard Partridge, for stepping into my life and mentoring me in business and life, I have learned so much from you and count you as a dear friend and mentor.

Zig Ziglar, for having an impact on the way I view life and for the foundational principle of "You can have everything in life you want if you will just help enough people get what they want."

Michael E. Gerber, for mentoring me through your book, *The E-Myth Revisited,* and for encouraging me to write a book... Here it is!

Tom Ziglar, the proud son of Zig Ziglar, for being a good friend and inviting me into your family and allowing me to carry on the message of Mr Ziglar! It really is an honor.

Mark Ehrlich, the man in black! If it weren't for you seeing something in me at the conference in Houston, and believing in me and my dreams even when I wasn't sure what they looked like...I would not have gone on to create my coaching and speaking career.

To my publisher, Barbara Dee, you are a gift from God... you have this ability to "get" me and understand and share my passion for Freedom in the lives of business owners. Thank you for taking on this project and believing in me and my message.

To everyone that has had an impact on my life—friends. clients, teachers (I'm sorry for being the overly mischievous kid in class—I was just trying to keep it fun!).

Last, but definitely not least, I acknowledge my Heavenly Father for giving me this message of freedom, passion in business, and love for people. My prayer is that people not only find freedom to succeed in business but also in their life, spiritually.

FOREWORD

By Howard Partridge

Dave Kauffman has a huge desire to make the world right.

He wants families to be close, he wants our country to be right, and he wants American business owners to be successful.

When I first got to know Dave Kauffman I saw a passion for entrepreneurship in him. This resonated with me as I was already coaching people and transforming businesses worldwide, but my career had not always looked that way.

In 1997, my entire life and business was about to change in ways I never knew would even be possible.

I had been in business for thirteen years. Thirteen LONG years. I felt like a slave to my business. I've always loved to travel, but when I did, much of that supposed "vacation" was spent on the phone talking to employees and customers back home. My business had become stressful, draining, and all-consuming.

Then, in 1997 I learned two secrets that changed everything. I read a book called *The E-Myth Revisited* by Michael E. Gerber.

It changed *everything* for me. The first secret I learned is that the one and only reason your business exists is to be a vehicle to help you achieve your L.I.F.E. goals.

If you don't have a vision for your life, if you don't know where you're going in life, then how will you build the right kind of business?

My acronym for L.I.F.E. is "Living In Freedom Everyday." There's no freedom in being a slave to your business. There's no freedom in being broke and in debt. There's no freedom in having difficult relationships with family, friends and employees.

The point is that you CAN have freedom. My friend and long time student, Dave Kauffman, gives readers a concise and practical plan in *Freedom To Succeed: The Diamond Mindset and Six Systems Needed For Business Success*.

Not only has Dave assimilated the teachings of Michael E. Gerber, Zig Ziglar and me, he has used this knowledge for nourishment of his own mind and creative process. He has integrated much into his own work with business owners, and has in fact created a new synthesis: the Business Diamond Assessment™ tool.

If you are in business for yourself and want the power to evaluate what really matters, you do not want to miss this assessment opportunity—you will find it in its entirety at the back of this book. It will require an investment of time and energy on your part, and it will be well worth it after you read the foundation for it, i.e., each chapter preceding the appendix.

Perhaps you picked up this book precisely because something about the word "freedom" in the title grabbed you and pulled you in. Everyone naturally seeks more freedom, but I find that business owners especially are people who value freedom. This desire has a lot to do with why someone starts a business in the first place. Yet, all too quickly, that wide-open sense of being free to create your future and direct your career path begins to constrict. This can be turned around by learning and applying the second secret I learned from Michael E. Gerber.

Michael E. Gerber, who is now a personal friend of mine, taught me that having SYSTEMS working for you in your business is the only way to operate with sustainable success.

Following the principles of getting clear on my life goals and building systems in my business (which includes building a phenomenal dream team) has helped me have more freedom AND success than I could have ever imagined.

Another way that Dave demonstrates his mastery of success principles is through his emphasis, explanation and examples of business systems. He has simplified the basic structure of a system to make it easy for you to create any system using his template. Being the generous guy that he is, he has included everything you need to develop systems here in *Freedom To Succeed*.

As I travel and speak to small business owners around the world, I find that most people don't understand that they ARE free—that they are FREE to succeed.

But in order to leverage that freedom, you have to understand what success is to you. You must understand WHY you are in business, WHY you want certain goals, WHY you are here on this earth.

What does success mean to you? You ARE free, but why does it matter? What will you do with that freedom?

With the right mindset and systems, you can achieve your greatest dreams, too. It is my privilege to introduce you to Dave and his unique, down-to-earth way of explaining these foundational principles for business success.

The greatest joy in the world is, to me, mentoring others. It is through mentoring Dave that I came to believe he would be one of those motivated people who have the determination and passion to never give up once they have a vision. So many people say they want to write a book, but most don't. When Dave told me he was writing a book, there was no doubt in my mind he would write one and that it would be published—and that it would reflect his authentic, often humorous, always caring character. I told him to feel free to draw on what he had learned over our years together. What could be more rewarding than to be quoted and acknowledged in an excellent book that gets the freedom message out to business owners?

You are not alone in your hunger for freedom. The Southwest airlines ad proclaims that "you are now free to roam the country." I say to you, "You are now free to succeed in life and business."

INTRODUCTION

The Last of the Free Range Children

My story has humble beginnings. Born on a large farm in Georgia, I was raised Amish-Mennonite. In many ways, my family and the people I knew adhered to a minimalist lifestyle. In stark contrast to a typical American child's life today, there were no stacks of video games in the boys' rooms, nor closets full of clothes or shoes in my sisters'. However, there was an abundance of clean air, fresh food, and a strong community bond, as you would imagine. What was the number one, most plentiful thing in my childhood? Freedom to roam.

Having the space, safety, and time to be a free-range child permanently shaped my core values and resides in me today as a burning passion. Freedom. Do all entrepreneurs and business owners have this motivating desire for freedom, however they define that for themselves? I say yes, and I wrote *Freedom to Succeed* for the very purpose of showing you how to gain and maintain freedom while succeeding in your business, no matter how demanding you feel your work is right now.

I have not spent too much time analyzing my early childhood years, but certain experiences I can recall do explain much of my personality as an adult, and why I strive for excellence in my roles as a husband, a Christian, a business owner, and a coach to entrepreneurs. I like to tell stories, especially ones

1

that I think help to illustrate an important point. This book not only includes key information and useful strategies, I share many stories and real-world examples to help you see the application and workability of all my material. And then, there may be a story or two just for the heck of it. Feel free to be amused.

I did not do too well in school, but one thing I excelled in was showing off and goofing around with the guys. For our own hilarity the other boys and I would shoot our pencils up into the drop tile ceiling. We would use our suspenders as slingshots to get the pencils to stick in, then get back to work immediately, pretending to have no clue what was going on. On one particular day, the big plan was to execute a simultaneous launch at exactly two o'clock.

The thing was, our teacher, Miss Miller, was not too observant. We often wondered if she was a little intimidated by us, considering all of the mischief we got away with. Either that or she just did not want to bother, so she turned a blind eye to our shenanigans. Of course, that meant we only pushed the boundaries further, taking advantage of every opportunity we had to see just how much we could get away with. It didn't always work.

So two o'clock came and we all shot our pencils into the air as quickly as we could so we could pretend we were working hard on our assignment before Miss. Miller looked up. Trying my hardest to suppress a smile, I heard the THUMP as the pencils hit the tile and stuck—all but mine.

Miss Miller looked up just in time to see my pencil bounce back onto my desk. I had not pulled my suspenders back far enough! I had to think quickly. With a shocked look on my face, I looked around and said, "Hey, who threw a pencil at me?"

Now, just imagine the scene. Miss Miller noticed many of the boys looking up (admiring their handiwork) and she looked up, too. We all had something extra to carry home that day—a note to our parents from Miss Miller.

Isn't it amazing how a young person can think of a million ways to both get into and out of trouble? In this predicament, my solution was simple: just flush the telltale note down the toilet and all will be fine with the world. Neither my teacher nor my mom would know any different, right?

Except, my teacher wouldn't let it go. The very next day she asked if I gave the note to my mom. I lied, of course, and told her that I did. I walked away, thinking that would be the end of it, but she asked me again the very next day. And again, I lied. I couldn't tell her the truth now, but I'm sure you can guess what happened next. This was back in the day when teachers could inflict a severe spanking if they thought it was deserved, and I received a blistering one.

The moment I got home that day, my mom and her scowl were waiting for me. Back when I had started school, my dad had made it clear what would happen to me if I ever got a spanking by my teacher: I would have one waiting for me at home as well! Two for the price of one, right?

If only I had read the note first, to see that my teacher wanted it to be signed by my mom and returned, then I could have saved myself a butt-load of trouble that day! (Note to self: 1. Don't lie. 2. Read the directions. 3. Cover your rear!)

I was naturally adventurous, and mischievous to a fault. But that's who I had to be. I was the youngest in the family, with four older brothers and an older sister. They were off doing older-aged things and chasing their own dreams, leaving me to myself. I had to generate my own excitement, which meant I was always busy creating new opportunities to explore. This independence and freedom to exercise my imagination later helped me have the right mindset to follow my business dreams and become a successful entrepreneur. Can you think of how your circumstances, behavior, and winning strategies early in life ended up helping you in your adult life, career, or business?

There were three things I always wanted to do in life: be an auctioneer, a pilot, and a veterinarian. I was a *take charge* type of kid, and as a seventh-grader, I enlisted my younger cousin to help me start an auction company. We called it Best Team Auction. The inspiration came from my uncle who owned an auction company called First Team Auction. Our goal? To be better than our uncle, of course!

We convinced our classmates to bring over personal items they were willing to sell. We gave them an opportunity to buy each other's goods. We brokered every deal, keeping a commission on what was sold. Decades later, I realized I still had a passion for the auction game and I graduated from the Florida Auction Academy on my 37th birthday.

Never underestimate the positive influence of a good uncle. One significant part of my life was inspired at an early age by another uncle who was not an auctioneer but a pilot. He would take me with him up in his small plane every opportunity he could. It was such a thrill and I became infatuated with flying. As a youngster, I would often make little airplanes to play with. As I got older, my paper plane obsession turned into a preoccupation with remote-controlled airplanes and helicopters.

One year, my dad hired a crop duster with a helicopter to spray our crops. I got to ride along in that helicopter as it flew up and down our fields. It was so exciting! I knew from that moment on that my goal was to be a pilot. I would even use my free time to study and memorize the checklist for my uncle's Cessna 182 RG. I shocked my father and brothers when I told them, "I can fly Uncle Richard's airplane!" and went down the whole checklist without missing a beat.

I was so proud of myself. Who else at such a young age could memorize the checklist to fly an airplane? At least in my mind that's what I thought. Every plane that passed overhead triggered my imagination. I had a dream to one day be a pilot and I pursued my goal with a passion. So, on my 21st birthday, I received my pilot's license!

Flying also taught me an important lesson about business. In Chapter 5, I share a "hard-earned lesson" story that might raise a few eyebrows, but serves to illustrate one of the most important things to understand and apply if you want the *Freedom to Succeed* type of business you deserve. Whether operating a plane or a company, there are things one MUST pay attention to, no matter what. In this book, I will show you exactly *what* those critical things are, *why* they are important, and *when* and *how* to monitor them.

Life growing up on the Amish farm was full of opportunities for adventure—there is just more time in the day when computers, television and video games are completely absent. I learned to be very entrepreneurial. If it wasn't running my own auction house, it was making and selling hundreds of gallons of lemonade with my sister at a stand by the side of the road. (Mom's "auto-correct" warns me not to exaggerate so much—change that to "gallons," not "hundreds of gallons.")

With no lack of experts on hand to teach me all the do's and don'ts about livestock, I learned how to raise pigs and calves for resale. It was through these working experiences that I determined I was better at working with people than I was with animals, machinery, or plants.

I am grateful for all that I learned on a farm, but knew from an early age that my calling was other than being a farmer. Believe me, I know farming is a business, but my business aspirations involved more interaction with people. I especially loved the idea of selling.

As a business owner you know that *nothing* happens until a *sale* happens. Thankfully, I followed my dream and learned everything I could about sales, about business, and most importantly, about people. In Chapter 4, I detail for you one of the most powerful tools I have ever found: DISC, a system for personality profile assessment. *Positive Personality Profiles* by Dr. Robert Rohm, a book which teaches you how to discover insights into personalities to build better relationships, is a great resource. I am certified with the DISC model of human behavior and have found it useful in many different applications, as I note in Chapter 4. DISC is used to easily discover how a person is "wired." There are different personality styles to understand, and that understanding will make all the difference in the world in your communication and relationship skills, both at work and home.

There are other resources I have found to be invaluable which I share with you in this book. My intention is to provide the best, most effective ideas to give you *Freedom to Succeed*. Way too much time is wasted trying to reinvent the wheel.

This book is hand-packed with wisdom from mentors and many examples and case studies from my own experience to help you quickly grasp the concepts and best practices to achieve *Freedom to Succeed*. Use the experiences, systems, and advice from experts who *know*, saving yourself costly mistakes, frustration, and maybe even the life of your business.

The primary company I own is where my heart lies: Empowering Small Business. We help business owners systematize their business so they can be more productive and spend more time on the things that are most important to them.

Exceptional Discipline Generates Excellence. EDGE Peer Groups (www.EdgePeerGroups.com) is the master program I developed, tested, and fine-tuned to be the best structure of support for business owners. This is the place where everything in this book becomes real: Goal achieving and problem solving with accountability, and mastermind solutions to business challenges.

Working with business owners from a multitude of industries and with varying business ages and sizes continues to provide the education I rely on. This is one reason I am known for giving practical vs. theoretical advice. I found that one of the first success principles I was advising every business owner on was to pause and take an honest and comprehensive look at his or her company. When you have a destination goal in mind, even if you have a detailed map and a guide to help you, your first step always needs to be to determine where you are now. That is what The Business Diamond Assessment™ tool is for, as I will explain a little later in this book.

While freedom, flexibility, and independence are strong desires for motivating people to work hard starting and building a business, these forces are soon diminished and often become substituted with pure stress infused with blood, sweat, and tears. Where's the fun in that?

Life is too short! Right now you can set your mind to the right channel to tune into freedom vs. being a slave to your business. The purpose of this book is to teach you the ONE mindset and the SIX keys to focus on to turn your business into the enjoyable, profitable entity you once imagined—without the struggle and stress that can creep in if you don't know how to design your business so there is simply no place for these to take root. The ONE mindset and SIX keys are all you need to gain the *Freedom to Succeed*.

Chapter 1

The Diamond Mindset

As a business owner, you already know it is a role with many costume changes. For a moment, imagine you are a doctor tasked with assessing your company's health. First, you would look at overall general health, but you only begin to get valuable information when you get specific. Examining different parts of the whole will tell you where the weaknesses and potential risks lie so that the causes for concern can be addressed.

Working with thousands of entrepreneurs and businesses (large and small) provided the experience and research results I needed to become better and better at diagnosing the health of a business and pinpointing the areas to improve. Whether you have a brand new business or one that has been established for years, you must look carefully at the key areas that you want in optimal health, i.e., functioning as you want, contributing all they are capable of contributing to the goal of having a successful business. These six areas are:

- Marketing
- Sales
- Procedures
- Office/Tracking
- Relationships
- Leadership

Within these six areas, I have identified the specific key indicators to focus us. Like in our doctor analogy, it is not enough to order lab work, you need to review the levels of certain elements such as Vitamin D and iron. Then you are armed with the clarity and information you need to make good decisions, provide what is missing, or investigate further. Because there are SIX areas of focus, the best diagram to illustrate my findings is diamond-shaped.

To help business owners quickly perform critical diagnostics and make better decisions, my team and I developed and now utilize a tool, The Business Diamond Assessment™. It has proven to be indispensable in my work, and, of course, I am eager to share it with you. Throughout this book you will find my best tips and coaching which led to The Business Diamond Assessment™ and I have included the diagram and the full collection of worksheets as Appendix I. A deeper discussion of the application and analysis can be found on my website: www.EdgePeerGroups.com.

Diamond Mindset + Systems = Freedom to Succeed

"The right mindset." We have all heard that having the right mindset is essential, whether you are a professional athlete, a person seeking a life partner, or an aspiring entrepreneur. There are useful practices including meditation, affirmations, or visualization which often help. But what are the specific *actions* to take? Attitude adjustment and positive thinking are not enough.

I found the answer by analyzing the actions of people who attained success and those who did not. I was obsessed finding the ONE thing that I could coach my business owner clients to focus on to guarantee their success.

What is the most important shift to make in order to break free of stress and grueling efforts and begin to thrive and enjoy the freedom you always wanted as your own boss? The answer has more to do with the heart than the mind—we should be talking about heart-set, not just mindset.

Too often I found that business owners were in love with the wrong thing. This comes about naturally, and that is why it is so prevalent. The love I am referring to is your love for what you do, what you provide customers or clients. A t-shirt designer loves to design, print and sell t-shirts. Well, perhaps they do not love to *sell* them, but they love it when customers buy them. Another example is the furniture store owner. With the help of two assistants, he is able to keep up with orders and fill his retail shop with quality pieces he is proud to put his name on. Sales, at least during the busy season, are good. Yet the revenue ceiling on these two companies is so low you have to duck just to walk into the operation.

MOST BUSINESS OWNERS ARE IN LOVE WITH THE WRONG THING...

DON'T BE IN LOVE WITH WHAT YOUR BUSINESS DOES— BE IN LOVE WITH

BUILDING A BUSINESS

THAT SUCCEEDS AT WHAT IT DOES.

—DK

Fewer than fifty percent of new businesses are still open after five years. Instead of being in love with what you do (i.e., provide "x"), you need to fall in love with *building a business* that provides "x."

I hope you are hearing a bell go off in your head as this should resonate. THIS IS THE KEY MINDSET TO UNDERSTAND, EMBRACE, AND PRACTICE. I said to a client, "You have been in love with making and selling pallets, and what I want for you is for you to fall in love with building a business that makes and sells pallets." I could see the proverbial bright lightbulb appear over his head!

With a "diamond mindset" you are passionate...about the right thing. The word "diamond" originates from a Greek word which means "unconquerable." Until the 15th century, kings were the only ones allowed to wear diamonds, as it was considered to be a symbol of strength and courage. Those who wore diamonds where thought to be invincible. Over the years, the diamond has become better known as the ultimate gift of love. This suggests the eternal nature of love, further going along with the Greek philosophy that the fiery brilliance of the diamond reflects the undying flame of love. My hope is that you will remember the diamond mindset: being in love with building a business that does what it was created to do... and does it brilliantly.

I am devoting myself to helping you, through this book, to develop the mindset and systems (those are the only two things you need!) so you will have everything you need, and *Freedom to Succeed*. I will show you exactly how to analyze your existing business, understand its strengths and weaknesses, and put each key area squarely on track for success. Read through the entire book, make notes, and re-read what speaks to you at this point in your life. I want to hear from you, especially if you need more information or encouragement. That is what I am here for. Read on!

Chapter 2

"The Cat and Milk Bowl" and Other Highly Effective Marketing Secrets

What do a cat and a milk bowl have to do with your business?

When I was a kid, I loved to go to my uncle's dairy farm and watch the farm hands milk the cows. Every morning and evening, before they left the barn they would pour plenty of fresh milk in a large flat bowl on the ground. The first time I saw this, I was quite curious about what I observed must be the last step in the cow-milking, but could not imagine why. Then I found out.

In no time at all, cats appeared, racing in from all corners of the farm. I will never forget that scene of fifteen cats of all colors stationed around the milk bowl—it was like a starburst of cats! The farm hands knew what the cats wanted, and the cats were not shy about showing their enthusiasm.

Years later I started my first company. As I was struggling to find customers, my mind was drawn back to the cats and the milk bowl. I started thinking about how that milk bowl was like a powerful magnet, attracting and satisfying the much-loved rodent dispensers, the farm cats. I wondered if my business was that attractive, and to whom? Who were my cats?

That's an excellent question to ask yourself if you're a business owner or in marketing. Ask: Who is my target market? What do they do, where do they go, how and what do they buy? What's their favorite eating establishment? Do they love milk? You get my point. You need to know your target market as much as you can!

In my cleaning company, we determined that our target market is women aged 40-60, who drive high-end cars and live in gated communities. You may be thinking that I am limiting myself and my company if I market only to this profile—not at all!

In a different analogy, let me ask: If your goal is to catch a lake trout, where is the only place you would go to fish? And, let's say you are not interested in lake trout; you really have your heart set on grouper. Would you not go precisely where you know the grouper hang out? Also, are you more likely to get a trophy fish with a net or a spear gun? You may not get as many fish with a spear but when you're very intentional and focused in your fishing (marketing), your chances of landing the big one increases greatly.

Now that I had defined my "cats" (my target market), I had to address the best way to attract and satisfy them. My mind shifted to the milk bowl. What was the milk bowl in this analogy? I asked myself a very important question: *Where does a 40-60 year old female that drives a high-end car and lives in a gated community go, often and on a regular basis?* (It is useful to brainstorm and note as many answers as you can.)

We came up with a list that included the delicatessen, the car wash, nail salons, hair salons....then it hit me! Hair salons were my magnet—my milk bowl! Why would I waste my time tracking down individuals in my target market when they already gathered at hair salons—specifically, salons which were in the local upscale neighborhoods?

The next step was to brainstorm about how to entice the cats to not only drink the milk they came for, but to become interested in another offering as well. Related to my business, I asked, "How do I attract the middle-aged female customers in hair salons to *my* company?" If only I could get the hair salon owner and employees to refer them to me... after all, they have my cats (target market) in their chairs all the time! And they do hair; my company cleans homes—so there is no competition, no reason not to send their customers to me. *But why would they?*

I had heard that people do business with those they KNOW, LIKE and TRUST. But nobody knew me, which certainly had to come before they could learn to trust me. I wasn't so sure if they even liked me....this was my first rodeo! So, what did I do? I made them like me!

I would walk in with a box of fresh donuts and a smile and say, "Good morning! I'm Dave with Got-A-Maid and I brought everyone donuts!" I would set the box down on the counter and start to walk out. *Every* time, someone would stop me before I got to the door. "You're WHO? And you brought us donuts?" I was their new best friend.

I was able to tell them about my service and share with them my mission statement for the company. I offered to clean their place for free just so they could see our quality and attention to detail. I would also tell them that I would be bringing them more donuts next month and—"Here are some 'referred by' cards. Just write your name on a card and give it to your favorite customer. We will reward you for every customer that you send to us."

Each hair stylist took a stack of cards, which they could turn into cash quite easily. "Oh, and by the way," I would add, "would it be okay if we send our high-end clients to you?" I collected their cards to pass on to customers. Now I was practically family!

Now you know how one of the most powerful marketing strategies in the world actually works. What are you going to do with it? Comprehensive teachings on this and similar sales concepts can be found in the work of international business coach, Howard Partridge (www.howardpartridge.com).

Much can be learned, too, through the teachings of the late Zig Ziglar. He became the top sales person in several organizations before striking out on his own as a motivational speaker and trainer. With lessons grounded in Christianity, Ziglar wrote over thirty books and amassed a following of millions who were encouraged by his lessons for success. He has had a profound influence on me. One of his famous sayings was that **you can have everything in life you want if you will just help enough other people get what they want.**

The lesson is to look for ways to give rather than focusing only on how to gain. The really neat thing about this approach is that any business can attract more (and more qualified) customers with a milk-bowl-and-cat system in place. Do you know who your target is?

Once you are clear on that, determine who they already connect with frequently. Build a relationship with those companies who already serve your target market and help them grow. The Bible says cast your bread upon the water and [in] many days it will come back to you! We are called to serve others, and that is the best way to build relationships—and when you build meaningful relationships, good things happen!

Do you have a good relationship marketing strategy only in order to attract *new* business? No, it should be employed with existing customers as well. When was the last time you cooked breakfast for your customers? You see, the number one mistake small businesses make is not marketing to their present and past customers. Taking care of your customers is the best form of marketing you can ever do.

According to Marketing Metrics, the probability of selling to a new prospect is 5-20 percent, while the probability of selling to an existing customer is 60-70 percent. Also, on average, loyal customers are worth up to 10 times as much as their first purchase. Of course, the most significant help to your business from existing customers comes from their willingness to refer others to you.

"Word of mouth" ...you've heard it hundreds of times. What do you need in order to have people talking about the greatness of your company? Great relationships! When I started my first business, I went to a friend of mine who had a very successful retail business serving local, high-end clients—the exact same customers I was looking for. I was not in competition, as my company provided a totally different service from what he did. Since we had the same target market, I came up with a strategy to get his customers to also be my customers.

To add value to his business, to him, and even to his family, I developed a deeper relationship with him, first by referring people to his store. I then asked him if I could put my business cards in his shop at the check-out counter (where every customer would see them). He agreed.

Before long, I started getting phone calls from people saying they picked up my card at that store. (By the way, *always* find out where someone heard about you so you can assess your marketing efforts.) It was working so well that I started to really focus on building relationships with other companies that had my ideal customers as their customers already. This is known as *relationship marketing* or *referral source marketing*.

Can you see that as well as being effective, it is also a highly efficient approach? Instead of going after one client, build a connection with a company that already has dozens of your ideal customers. Imagine what could happen when you build relationships with enough people and companies that know, like, and trust you, and are willing to send their customers to you.

I started out telling you about a simple milk bowl and the cats that were drawn to it. Use that image to help you as you define your ideal customers and the best strategy to attract them. Feel free to contact me about my personalized coaching and success strategy programs for small businesses like yours.

Marketing is essential with any business venture if you hope to make money. If people don't know you exist, how can they find you? And if they can't find you, you're simply not making the sales you need to be successful. While some marketing will offer results, the right kind of marketing can be the difference between mediocre sales and taking off like a rocket.

The reality is, good marketing is like a candle in a dark cave. It stands out so much, every part of you will be drawn to it. Your eyes and your attention will be drawn towards the light! It doesn't take much to convince yourself that you NEED this product, nor can you live without it. It resonates with you. It identifies your needs. It educates.

So what's the big secret for marketing the right way? It's all about targeting the right crowd. Your marketing should attract your target audience, not every single person you can get the message to. Think about it like this: a bug zapper was designed to attract bugs. That's what it was built to do. It's not meant to attract kangaroos or crocodiles.

Resources are finite, and attempting to attract people who do not fit the target audience is just like setting your money on fire. Why? People buy things for two reasons:

1) For gain. They want to raise their personal brand and improve their image. To impress. Maybe it's for the girl they have a crush on or to secure a promotion. Maybe it entertains them in ways other products cannot. The purchase is made with one thing in mind: If I buy this product, what will it do for me?

We often do and buy things because it improves the way other people see us. How many times have you purchased an item simply to build a relationship with someone? I've had clients buy from me to have a relationship with me, and likewise I've bought and attended seminars to maintain a relationship with others. Whatever we purchase, it's done with gain in mind.

Take Rolex as an example. Why should you buy a Rolex? Well, as the top watch brand in the world, owning a Rolex has a bit of prestige added to it. It's expensive and says something about you. If you own a Rolex, it screams class and tells the world you're an important person. So what is Rolex's message? "A Rolex will never change the world. We leave that to the people who wear them."

Their message is, if you want to be a person of influence, a world changer, a SOMEBODY, then buy a Rolex. This is what you buy to gain something.

2) To avoid pain. We don't purchase life, health, and car insurance because we have a ton of money lying around and have to buy SOMETHING. And there's nothing fun or

sexy about an insurance policy. What about home protection systems? I live in Florida and it's a MUST to have hurricane shutters. Oh yes, there's just something about a large, bulky, non-see-thru shutter to make my house look great!

What about dental care? Do you spend big money on a root canal because the dentist is a good friend of yours and you want to support his practice? I doubt it, but you get the point. If you don't make the investment now, you will definitely feel the pain later! We buy things to avoid feeling that pain. Take a look at this advertisement copy:

> Ted works very hard. Ted has everything.
> Ted finally retires, as does his disability policy.
> Ted decides to go fishing. Ted slips on a rock.
> Ted loses everything. Don't be like Ted!

The ad then shows Ted in a whole-body cast unable to move. So why do we spend a lot of money on insurance? It can almost seem like a waste of money until you're in Ted's position. All it takes is one moment like that, while completely unprotected, to become overwhelmed with hospital bills and eventually lose everything you worked for.

When you take these two points into account, you should ask yourself what your message is. What problem are you solving? How can you make people's lives better? Why should anyone buy what you're selling? When you do this, it makes your marketing much more effective.

Howard Partridge, my friend and mentor, says that when you market, it should educate, entertain, and engage.

You should EDUCATE your target market on their gain or pain points and how they should depend on your product to soothe their needs.

You should ENTERTAIN with your message so you can hold their attention and intrigue them.

And finally, your marketing should ENGAGE them by making them think. Get in their head by asking questions they are forced to answer.

This is the difference between simple marketing and good marketing. Simple marketing just lets the world know your service or product exists, but it goes no further than that. It may bring in a few sales, but what does it actually do to target and engage? With good marketing, you are letting them know WHY they should buy and what you offer that no one else does. How do you meet their needs in a way they can't get from someone else down the street?

Experiential Marketing

I love the television hit show *Shark Tank*, where real entrepreneurs pitch their idea or company to potential investors. In one particular episode, Mark Cuban (billionaire entrepreneur and investor) made the largest deal in *Shark Tank* history with Ten Thirty-One Productions. This pitch was from a company that specialized in producing and creating live horror shows. Cuban offered two million dollars for a 10% stake in the company. Why was he willing to make the biggest deal in the show's history? As Mark Cuban himself explained, he sees entertainment becoming more experiential in the near future.

What exactly is experiential marketing? It's essentially offering something that people can experience in real life. You can touch it, feel it, and view it in a real physical space. As social media continues to explode, so do the attempts from marketers to turn marketing into an experience. Any product (from movies to cars to insurance) can be marketed with the intention to make the brand have a real, tangible presence in the lives of the consumers. This can be done either in person or through digital media, with platforms including Facebook, Twitter, Instagram, and YouTube.

The question you need to ask yourself is: if the goal of your marketing is to persuade while entertaining, how would your sales improve if you were to start giving your target market a true experience? It is a "above and beyond" approach to marketing.

A good example of experiential marketing is a disaster restoration company in California that invested in a BBQ food truck. First they do their homework to identify their target market in their geographic area. They then go around to those various companies in the area who are in the position to buy the services they offer and cook bar-b-que for the decision-makers and their staff. Talk about an incredible opportunity and experience that other companies will always remember! It's this kind of creative, experiential marketing that will put them head-and-shoulders above the competition.

Let's look at more examples of experiential marketing. In one of my companies, we use a payroll service that handles the payroll in my company. The owner of that payroll service likes to take me fishing from time to time. How awesome is that?! When other payroll companies come asking for my business, I always reply with the question: "Do you have a boat?" Granted, that is not the only criteria I use in selecting a vendor, but since my payroll company does provide high quality service at a fair price, the bonus experience clinches the deal.

I once met a dentist who had a massive tooth. Okay, actually it was a character costume of a giant tooth. He would hire a person to wear it in schools and libraries while reading to the kids. Can you imagine a giant tooth reading you a story? That is an awesome idea right there, even if you are not a kid! This inspired me to create a giant vacuum for my Got a Maid? company for the same purpose. Seriously, have you ever had a large vacuum or tooth read to you? They would then hand out bookmarks and other materials with my logo on them, sharing with the kids why it's important to read. Talk about having an experience!

One of the best examples is a painting company that invests (not "spends") a lot of time teaching senior citizens how to use iPads and iPhones. You may be asking yourself why a painting company would teach seniors how to do that, but it's really brilliant marketing! You see, their company has determined that retired seniors who own their own home are ideal prospective customers. Also, the most qualified target customers are fairly affluent, i.e., able to afford high-end technology (even if they can't use it!).

Offering these classes gives the painting company an "in." Imagine you have become extremely frustrated in your attempts to use your smart phone or tablet and do not have any grandchildren nearby to come over and help. But you do have this nice volunteer, Jim, sent by Joe the Painter, willing to spend time with you, absolutely free, to teach you how to use your iPad. He even sets you up to Skype with your favorite granddaughter. Jim seems almost like one of the family because he has solved a problem very personal to you. When you need a painter, you call that wonderful company that sent you Jim to save the day. You call Joe the Painter. Period.

Put Marketing Into Action

When was the last time you cooked breakfast for your current customers? You see, the number one marketing mistake small businesses make is not marketing to current and past customers. Taking care of your customers is the best form of marketing you will ever do. If you give your customers an amazing marketing experience, do you think that they might just tell a few people?

Of course they will! They will tell everyone they know, not just about your great product, but the wonderful customer service they experienced. It means a lot to a customer to know they are valued and cared for. What happens is word of mouth. Word of mouth is THE best form of advertisement. Suddenly you don't just have to listen to an ad tell you how great something is, you get to experience it first hand with a real customer who has a lot of great things to say.

Zig Ziglar once said, "You can have everything in life you want if you will just help enough other people get what they want." The Bible says, "Give and it will be given back to you." Karma says, "What goes around, comes back around." My uncle said, "Scratch my back, I'll scratch yours." The Business Network International (BNI) slogan, *Givers Gain*, is another example. I could go on and on, but the mantra is the same.

The great relationships you need now and down the road can be started (by you!) with a simple act of generosity. Back when I opened my first business, I had a friend who ran a successful business servicing high-end customers. I wanted the same exact clientele, and (this is important) my friend and I were not in competition with each other—my services were completely different from his. I very much wanted to tap into the customer base he had already established. So what did I do?

I made sure I added value to him, his family, and his business. In the interest of developing a deeper relationship with him, I started to refer people I knew (including the few customers I had) to his store. When I asked him if I could set up my business cards near his checkout line, he had no issues with it! I gave, he gave. Reciprocity is a natural phenomenon.

It wasn't long before I started getting phone calls from people saying they saw my card and they would like to learn more about what I do. We started getting so many referrals from that one relationship that I started building relationships with other companies with the same goal in mind! This is called relationship marketing, or referral source marketing.

To help sweeten the pot, you can offer a company a "free trial" so they can try out what you do. You can do like I did, and reward the other company for sending you referrals. It is a whole lot easier for someone to partner up with you if they know and trust what you do. Once you have built that relationship up enough, you will be sharing tons of customers between each other and it will only grow from there.

Have you ever gotten so busy that you neglected an important relationship? If we are telling the truth, we all have. All that work to attract a particular kind of person into our sphere and then make the effort to connect and build trust...but is the bridge we built permanent and maintenance-free? Never. Ongoing committed action is required.

Ongoing? How often does a relationship need attention? What kind of committed actions are best? Examples of committed actions are a phone call, email letter, newsletter or blog with valuable content, invitation to have coffee or lunch, giving business or referrals to them, stopping in their place of business, gifting tickets to a game or other event, or sending a handwritten note of appreciation. A combination of committed actions is the smart way to go. Being consistent with at least one or more actions is crucial, so you need a structure in place to insure key relationships are never neglected. The only way to be sure no one is left out and that everyone is consistently engaged is to use a system.

Chapter 3

The Systems Will Set You Free

How did the 60-foot tall live oak tree on my street get there? Through one of nature's systems. One thing we can learn from God's hand is the necessity, structure, and value of systems. For running a business, nothing can replace the benefit of having good systems.

"They've got it down to a science." This means a particular group has a task mastered so well that when they do it, it is done quickly, without error, and even with style! I am going to show you exactly how to transform the tasks of running your business with systems that will allow you to operate with the confidence and efficiency possible when you "have it down to a science."

As you go about your day, you may not realize how much systems (or lack of them) impact your daily life. When I think about my childhood growing up on a farm, I realize that systems were everywhere. In fact, all agriculture consists of sets of systems.

How does a farm attempt to duplicate nature's systems? In more ways than we can name. Just for the crucial task of water application in order to supply water requirements not satisfied by rainfall, there are at least ten different man-made methods. Examples are irrigation using perforated pipe, partial surface flooding, and spray sprinklers. Any one system for water application includes equipment, a procedure, and a schedule—exactly like any system you can set up to help your business handle crucial tasks.

Having and using systems is especially important in business, and successful companies all have them. One can say that McDonald's has a fairly amazing plan to maximize profits. Have you ever wondered how they can put out hamburgers so quickly? By the time you put in your order and pull around to the window, your whole meal is ready to go.

That's because McDonald's has a proven system to get food to their customers as quickly as possible. Recently, the fast food chain has been testing one-minute-or-less guarantees to help generate more interest – and profits – during the lunch hour. Whether or not they will fully adopt the policy, time will tell. But as a company, they have every detail of their operations down to a science. You have someone on grill, a few people working the veggies, someone else warming the bread. It's an assembly line designed to crank out burgers at supersonic speed. Using a system guarantees consistency—my wife affirms this by saying McDonald's food is *consistently* awful.

The great thing about having a system in place is its ability to set you free! What I mean by that is, the whole operation takes care of itself. The workers go in knowing what to expect each day. They know they should do the same thing every day, whether they are the ones flipping the burgers or dunking the fries in hot oil—for *exactly* three minutes and ten seconds (add twenty-four seconds for nuggets). It is the same process over and over again. Once trained on the system, they know what the expectations are. And once you have someone there overseeing the whole operation, what else is there for you to do? Absolutely nothing! What can be more brilliant than that?

ORGANIZE AROUND BUSINESS FUNCTIONS, NOT PEOPLE.

BUILD SYSTEMS WITHIN EACH BUSINESS FUNCTION. LET THE SYSTEMS RUN THE BUSINESS AND PEOPLE RUN THE SYSTEMS.

—Michael E. Gerber

Back when I started my first company, I had the energy and passion that fueled it to get off to a good start. Soon after, when the U.S. economy tanked, my wife and I both got laid off at our "day jobs." Now our small business became our entire lifeline. Unfortunately, I had lost my initial enthusiasm, had become frustrated, and felt trapped.

I desperately wanted to grow the company and bring in more revenue, but to do that meant adding more frustration into the mix. I was open to suggestions and that's when my friend Dave stepped in. He suggested that I go with him to a conference in Houston, Texas. He thought I would find it helpful, but I just couldn't afford to go. With having a business to run during one of the most economically trying times in America's history, it didn't seem like a good idea.

But I went anyway. I want to mention that this is an important part of the story, because if I had not gone, you wouldn't be reading this book!

The moment the conference started at 8 AM, the speaker asked, "Do you remember why you started your business? Was it to make money, or to have more free time?" I started to think to myself…*that's exactly why I started my own business.* He continued: "How is that working out for you?"

"Not very well," I admitted to myself under my breath. I had another thought…that this conference had just started. This guy has barely been on stage five minutes and he was already getting under my skin and pushing my buttons. How was I going to endure two more days of this? But I decided to give the guy a chance and it was one of the best decisions of my life.

As he got into the bulk of his message, the speaker started talking about a business that was predictable, profitable, and considered a turnkey. I immediately knew that was exactly what I wanted; a company that was able to run and operate without me having to be there 24/7, one that I could trust to keep humming along, even when I occasionally unplugged myself. By the end of the conference, hope was beginning to seep back into the picture. Finally, I started to picture just how amazing my company could be.

Thanks to that speaker—who by the way was Howard Partridge, who later became my mentor—I had an epiphany that you should start to consider as well: I'm in full control of my company. I made all the decisions on how it runs. I got to choose how my dream and vision would be fulfilled. Even a small company could have a mission statement and a set of goals that are to be achieved. Of course! They were MY goals. And the reason why I was so frustrated all the time was because of how I designed my company. As the architect of the business, I get to design the ideal business I want. And, just like in nature, my ideal business needs good systems in place.

YOUR BUSINESS IS PERFECTLY DESIGNED

TO GET THE RESULTS YOU ARE NOW GETTING.

IF YOU WANT DIFFERENT RESULTS, YOU MUST CHANGE THE WAY YOU DO THINGS.

— Tom Northup

Options Strategy (Not "Exit Strategy")

You want to create a business that can thrive without you, even if you have no intention of stepping back or selling the business any time soon. Building a sellable business gives you options, i.e., FREEDOM. Even though it is sometimes hard to imagine that you will ever want to turn over a business you worked so hard to build, there are many reasons for wanting to design your business so that it would be highly attractive to others. These motivations include the not-so-unusual idea that you may want to start another business, or you may want more time for yourself, or you may be counting on your company as your best shot at a comfortable retirement. No matter what, I guarantee you will sleep better at night knowing that you *could* sell your business if you wanted to or needed to.

If It's Done More Than Once, It Probably Needs a System

Unless you bought a McDonald's franchise, you get to create your own systems to run your business. They are as imperative to your business success as any other factor. What if you didn't have a system for invoicing or getting paid by customers? Accounting systems are the most obvious ones you need, but any area that warrants a system should have one.

31

Having effective systems is the only practical way to manage the important details of your operation. These details are found in lower-level subsystems. For example, your marketing system may have a subsystem called lead generation. The lead generation system could have subsystems such as Facebook, email campaigns, or direct mail. Systems and subsystems are the ASSETS that deliver consistent results, even when you're not around.

Here are a few examples of small business systems. Which ones apply to your business?

1. Prospect Follow-up System
2. Sales Tracking System
3. Contact List Management System
4. Social Media Marketing System
5. Hiring System
6. Billing System
7. Key Account Management System
8. Shipping System
9. Order Fulfillment System
10. Employee Training System

For those who manufacture or sell products of others, you will need to put together a distribution and delivery system to get that product from where it originates to the buyers and end users. You may already have a method of doing this, but I am asking you to challenge yourself to improve your system of delivery to be even more efficient and cost-effective. The elements of technology you implemented five years ago could very well stand to be upgraded or replaced if the ROI (return on investment) makes sense. Make a note to yourself to have your current delivery system technology reviewed if you have not done so recently.

Having an excellent distribution and delivery system in place is crucial for the success of your business. Without it, you could have serious problems with cash flow, customer satisfaction, and limited business growth. With it, you will gain much advantage in your *Freedom to Succeed.*

When designing or revamping your distribution system (or any system, actually) you must look at costs. Time, labor, and expense have to be analyzed so that once your system is in place you can trust it to help your business function and grow, not spin it in the wrong direction. Typical questions you should be asking are: What are the costs involved? Can I afford to offer free shipping? Can I afford a large shipping and receiving team to keep up with regular demand? Is international shipping even cost effective? There's a lot to consider.

With the explosion of online sales through the Internet tycoon, Amazon.com, it is more challenging than ever to compete. Amazon has a membership program where, for an annual fee, the customer can order everything from computers to hot sauce to designer shoes—with NO shipping charges! Consumers are getting spoiled. An online coffee bean company came to the conclusion "if you can't beat 'em, join'em" and now offers free shipping. Their customers demanded it!

But, Mr. Coffee Bean was smart: he analyzed his shipping costs very carefully before changing his policy to offer free shipping to customers. First, he found that he could negotiate with UPS and get a better price from them, based on quantity. Then, he found ways to raise his prices here and there to offset the additional expense for shipping that he would no longer simply pass on to the customer. Then, after determining the right "minimum order" amount to make "free shipping" work, he implemented his offer and shored up his competitive position. Your delivery system is one of the most important places where you must know your numbers.

While we are looking at your delivery system (and every business has one, even if it is a service company) let us take note of one fantastic benefit to getting this system right. Think about it: your delivery system may be the very best place to look for a USP (unique selling point). A unique selling point (or proposition) is the factor presented as the reason one brand of product or service is different from and better than that of a competitor.

As Theodore Levitt, author and professor at Harvard Business School, said, "Differentiation is one of the most important strategic and tactical activities in which companies must constantly engage." Quick example: There are six Chinese restaurants in town in addition to yours. All but two of them offer a take-out menu as an option. Only one of the seven—yours—offers delivery service. Because you figured out a cost-effective way to differentiate your business, you will own 100% of the market share of customers wanting their food delivered to their door.

By the way, a system is never written in stone. Once your company achieves a certain momentum, you may find that it is difficult to scale your business based on your original product, pricing, or distribution model. In order to break free, you must find ways to support and augment your existing business with new strategies and upgraded systems.

A business system may be as simple as a checklist created in an hour or two. However, more complex systems can take days or even weeks to implement.

If you do not already have a Systems Manual with your existing systems written out and organized, use the format below.

You should decide on your major categories and then list the subsystems within that main system. For example, your Marketing System will have several subsystems like Lead Generation or Affiliate Program.

Once you have the system in place, it starts to do the work for you. As you write each part of the system, add it to a systems binder for easy access.

The systems will all be listed in one computer file (such as in MS Word) for easy revisions and additions, but I recommend also printing out the pages to put in a three-ring binder. In fact, you may want to create a duplicate manual to take home as a back-up—it's that valuable.

A Proven Template For Your Systems Manual

Some systems are short and sweet, while others are complex. Here is a simple four-component format to help set up your systems, whether the details fit on one page or take several:

NAME OF SYSTEM

SET-UP

SCHEDULE

PROCEDURE

The page(s) for your Systems Manual will be consistent:

THE _____ SYSTEM

Revision date: _____

SET-UP:

[State where the supplies, information and tools needed to use this system are kept. List anything needed at hand to complete this system procedure.]

_____

_____

_____

_____

_____

SCHUEDULE:

[Note how often and when this system should be used. Every Friday? The 15th of each month? Any time a call comes in requesting product information? At the close of each quarter?]

_____

_____

_____

_____

_____

PROCEDURE:

[List each and every step, in order, including all materials, information, resources, people or data required to complete the procedure.]

_____

_____

_____

_____

Can you identify systems you already have in place? For example, if you wrote down your existing Lead Follow-up System in the four-part outline, you would have your first page of your Systems Binder.

If you have someone working for you who is responsible for a multi-step, repeatable task, ask him or her to write up what is done to perform that task using the four-part format. If several systems are used, ask that each one be recorded. (You don't have to underline the fact that if that person leaves the company, you will be in infinitely better shape to train a replacement once you have a Systems Manual.)

As you begin to look at all the systems already in use in your business, you will notice three things:

You will see where a multi-step task is being accomplished, but the process is sloppy. Without a written system, including the step-by-step procedure, there is little chance of it getting done consistently, efficiently, and cost-effectively.

Other areas will seem to be running like a Swiss clock. This is where you need to document the set-up, frequency, and steps to a well-working system already in place. This will enable you to get the task back on track quickly in case that "clock" stops keeping perfect time.

Gaps and bottlenecks may also show up. This is where to analyze what is missing, and develop a complete system to improve productivity and workflow. If you don't, it is only a matter of time until things will grind to a halt. Just like in nature, if part of a system is missing, the fruit withers and dies on the vine.

EXAMPLE:

This system is the responsibility of a part-time office assistant in a busy doctor's office. The business website has a free ebook offered in order to attract visitors, and to showcase the doctor's special expertise.

In order to download the free ebook, the website visitor must enter their name and email address. This information can be printed out as a report so the contact can be put into a follow-up system. Between 50-100 ebook downloads occur each week. The doctor does not want to pass up the opportunity to connect with people who visit his website and take the time to download his ebook. The only way to insure consistent follow-up is with a system.

THE EBOOK DOWNLOAD FOLLOW-UP SYSTEM

SET-UP:

To perform this process, you will need the most recent <u>report</u> containing names and email addresses collected from ebook download requests on our website.

You will be cross-referencing these names with our <u>patient database</u>. On your office computer, open the patient database. You also need to open <u>Doctor Smith's email</u> account set up for the purpose of patient communication. You need two EBOOK F-U letter templates, one for patients, one for non-patients.

SCHUEDULE:

Every Wednesday morning, before noon.

PROCEDURE:

1. Print out the ebook download contact list.
2. Using the patient database, note whether the contact is a patient or a new contact.
3. Using the template for patients, fill in the name and send the P-EBOOK F-U letter.
4. Using the template for non-patients, fill in the name and send the N-EBOOK F-U letter.
5. On the report, circle any contact whose email bounces back.
6. Give the report with notations to the office manager.

This is obviously an example of a fairly simple process, part of the larger marketing system. Some of the process has already been automated; some parts that could be are not yet automated. This is typical. You'll want to look at your operations and see where automating another step here and there makes sense. By the way, it is IMPOSSIBLE to automate chaos! So every time you create a system for your Systems Manual, you are forwarding the process of streamlining and setting the stage for easier automation in the future.

IT IS NOT POSSIBLE TO AUTOMATE CHAOS.

BUT A MANUAL SYSTEM CAN BE EASILY AUTOMATED AT ANY TIME.

—DK

With systems, you get your best workflow. With flow, you get FREEDOM. Here is one example that helped me realize the true value of systems and, in fact, shaped my thinking about this book and what freedom for a business owner actually looks like.

My phone rings and it's my office manager. "David," she said, "I don't know how to tell you this—but today is my last day."

I must have misunderstood. For a moment, I thought she had told me she was leaving the job, and with no notice. That could not be, so I asked her what she meant. "The city called me," she continued. "They said the child services job is mine if I want it." I then remembered that she had gone to school for that career and was hoping an opening would become available. She told me that she had, of course, accepted it while telling them she would need to give a two-week notice to me. But they said she needed to accept it that day, begin the job the next day, or they would move on to the next person.

I told her that I would never hold her back from her dream, and it was okay. And then it hit me that my wife and I (the only other people who had a hand in managing the company) were leaving for Honduras in three weeks. (In a cartoon of myself, a huge YIKES! now appears.)

So the next day we started looking for her replacement. We searched and searched. Finally, one week before we were supposed to leave, we hired somebody…not telling her that we were leaving in one week and that she would be running the show on her own! We started training her, working with her side-by-side for three days. Then I told her, oh by the way, we're leaving for Honduras next Monday.

Her eyes got huge as her face flushed with panic then anger. "Why didn't you tell me?" she wanted to know. I was honest with her, telling her that I needed her to trust me…that initially she would not have wanted to come on board if she knew what was coming up, but that I was confident after working with her a few days that everything would be fine. Before she could protest further, I handed her our thick, navy blue Systems Manual. I told her not to worry about a thing—everything she needed to know about running the office was in this manual. Everything.

We gave her our contact information and left the country. The whole week we were in Honduras, there was not one phone call. Not one email. I was worried, thinking that she had quit, locked up, gone home, and I was out of business.

I got back from Honduras and walked into the office—and there she was, pleasantly smiling and very relaxed. She said it was the most amazing experience. "Every time I had a question or got stuck, I just opened the book and there was my answer."

This was one of the millions of times I find myself grateful for my wife's partnership—she had worked diligently with the previous office manager to set up our complete Systems Manual. If you do not have one, do not delay. Start by listing your existing systems and recording the Name, Set-up, Frequency, and Procedure for each, just like in the example earlier in this chapter.

Chapter 4

Sales, the 110% Rule, and Dealing with "D"

Have you ever noticed that no matter how many conversations occur, or stacks of papers get filed, or how many full-out flurries of activity take place, these may or may not result in a single sale or one dollar of revenue for your business? Sales is where the heart of the business is beating, driving all other functions—or it isn't. Sales is where a company thrives and is fruitful, or withers on the vine and dies.

The way I want business owners to think about sales is with respect, first of all. The role of the salesperson in your organization, even if right now that only points to you, is as crucial (or more so) than any other. This is the junction where company meets customer and something happens. If it's just a friendly introduction, that's involvement. If a sale happens, that's commitment. The difference between ham and eggs? The chicken was involved, the pig was committed.

The commitment from you must start way before the sale to the customer happens. Building trust and laying the groundwork for your offer is part of sales, and must not be skipped over as if getting in front of the prospective customer is the only, or the most important goal.

In my workshops and EDGE peer groups, we discuss trust extensively and one of my maxims is:

"Trust starts with your ability...Ability needs Accountability... Accountability builds Credibility...

Credibility builds Trustability."

Let's face it: if potential clients do not trust you, you are going to have an incredibly difficult time getting them to engage with you. They would instead rather spend their time, energy, and money on your competition, who they perceive as meeting their needs better than you do. Building trust with potential customers ALWAYS means you have a better chance of being the preferred choice, and of closing the sale.

You may be thinking that people should readily trust you since, after all, you are trustworthy, right? Does it work for you if someone (especially someone who is in a position to sell you something) says the words to you, "trust me"? No. Naturally, trust must be earned. The good news is that once you understand how trust can be built, you can use efficient and effective methods to do so.

There are specific commitments you need to make, and have your sales staff make, that you can learn as your secrets to effective sales.

Commitment Secret #1: Talk Less and Listen More.

When you are new to the game and trying to build a relationship, oftentimes it can feel a bit forced. Grateful for the brief chance to engage your prospective customer, you are eager to impress and "sell them." You want them to know all about your amazing product or service. How could you convert them from a prospect to a customer without actually talking about what you do? Surely they are engaging with you only to hear all about features and benefits so they can make a buying decision. Yes? NO!

If you are the one doing all the talking, how well are you listening to the needs of your potential customer? And if you are not listening, how can you provide solutions to their needs? The best way to approach any business deal is to ask questions and then listen. Take notes. If you think you aren't clear on something, ask more questions. Note: "LISTEN" and "SILENT" have the exact same letters. As Zig Ziglar so aptly said, "Telling ain't selling."

Let's say you have been in the same business for long enough that you have a good handle on the most pressing needs of your target customers. You have asked questions and heard very similar answers from so many people that you understand a prospect's concerns and needs after he speaks for one minute—or sometimes before he even opens his mouth. Do you still need to ask questions and listen carefully to what they tell you? Absolutely. Your job is to show that person that you hear and understand their needs. That is the first step to becoming someone they trust and someone who can influence them. Joe, the guy in the diner, can attest to this.

The guy in the diner? Yes. One day a nuclear physicist named Walt was sitting at the lunch counter at the local diner when his left foot suddenly cramped up so intensely that he dropped his fork full of potato salad. He reached down to where his feet rested on the stool's footrest and started to vigorously rub his left foot in an attempt to remedy the charley horse.

Joe, the guy working behind the counter who had served the Blue Plate Special to Walt five minutes earlier, came over to inquire. "Muscle cramp," Walt said, tilting his face up to the countertop as he continued to bend over and massage his foot.

"Is the spasm in your foot or calf?" Joe asked.

"Left foot. But sometimes it happens in my right foot. Never my calves."

"Do you get the cramps only when you are sitting or lying down?"

"Well, yes. That does seem to be the only time they come on."

"Do you drink at least a glass of water every couple of hours?"

"No, I get busy with my nuclear physics calculations and go all day with no food or water."

"How about at night?" Joe asked. "Do you get muscle cramps at night?"

"Well, now that you mention it…"

Can you guess what happened next? That's right! A nuclear physicist took medical advice from a guy in a diner. Joe had become a "trusted advisor" simply by asking the right questions and listening attentively, causing Walt to believe that he really understood him and his problem. If you can demonstrate that you understand someone's problem, perhaps articulating it even better than they can, you will have a great deal of influence on them.

When you are asking questions, you are in control of the conversation. Yet you never want to come across as their interrogator, firing off one question after another. The entire purpose of your questions should be to elicit information that reveals the person's most pressing problems and needs—so you can craft and offer a perfectly-suited solution (or be honest and tell them you cannot). For this to occur, you need a repertoire of strategic questions. That way, you can avoid asking dozens of questions and not finding any pearls. Your list of questions will evolve as you discover how to be strategic in this part of your Sales System.

As we discussed in Chapter 3, having a system in place for every key function in your organization is critical. In the area of sales, you will need several sub-systems in your overall Sales System. A tractor runs in order to produce the result of tilling the soil, for example, but it will not run without a drive train, an exhaust system, a fuel pump and other systems working in tandem.

Sub-systems for sales may include: lead generation, reputation management, getting referrals, soliciting existing customers, appointment setting, closing the sale, and follow-ups.

Using a system consistently will allow you to gauge your results and see what is working to accomplish your goals of building trust, creating relationships with your target market, attracting prospective customers, and closing sales.

Commitment Secret #2: Be Informative and Honest. Always give 110% of yourself in everything you do. That includes being completely honest about what you can deliver. Again, it is not about talking and talking and talking. Once you listen to your customer's needs, then show them what you can do and how you provide them with value. Be authentic and relatable.

The sad truth is that there is too much dishonesty in every market. Snake oil salesmen fill the landscape with promises they never fulfill and mess it up for everyone else. You can stand out in your market by being honest and living up to what you say you can deliver. Otherwise, you will gain a bad reputation and that is often too high a barrier to overcome. Going above and beyond is always appreciated and will attract new customers. The prime directive in your company must be to be honest with prospects and customers and keep all commitments.

In the 1980s, believe it or not, not everyone had a computer. (And, incredibly, there was no Internet for us to use and we still managed to get through school and be productive in our jobs.) But the PC popularity explosion was happening and it was an era when demand for computer expertise and service far exceeded supply. Unfortunately, this often led to computer companies treating customers poorly as they were too busy and too in demand to care about customer service. A business that had just automated their operations would have computer problems which caused huge breakdowns in productivity. If they could not get back up and running quickly, it was very frustrating and expensive. In many cases, however, a computer technician who was called to come fix the problem would show up hours late or not at all.

A friend of mine in Atlanta used this enormous problem that companies were experiencing to set her computer service company head and shoulders above the competition. Her technicians had the same certifications as other service providers, but her secret to (tremendous) success was her tag line. The white company vans were painted with the cobalt blue logo and:

PLANET COMPUTER SERVICES
— WHERE PROMISES ARE MADE AND KEPT.

No other computer service company was even talking about "promises" much less making such a bold commitment to keeping them. Being honest and reliable were key to influencing businesses to hire and retain long-term customer relationships with Planet Computer Services. Companies were not about to go elsewhere, once they finally found a service provider who would consistently show up when they said they would and keep their commitments. There was no reason to stop doing business with a trustworthy company, plus the customers felt comfortable and unusually eager to tell others about their positive experience.

Commitment Secret #3: Be True to Your Passion. Something that potential customers love to see is passion. Drive. Confidence. When you have passion, you absolutely LOVE what you do and can't see yourself doing anything else. It is that attitude that will take you far versus seeming like you are only in it for the money; it is just a job.

Have you ever gone to a fast food restaurant and noticed the faces of the workers there? With rare exceptions, there is no enthusiasm. All they care about is watching the clock so they can go home. But every so often, you find one who is in a great mood. And that great mood is contagious, right? It sticks with you for awhile.

You are a living example of the services you offer your customers. What you offer can potentially make their lives more enjoyable, less stressful, or more fulfilled. As discussed before, a person wants to buy from you because they are looking to avoid pain or achieve gain. By meeting their needs, you are making their lives better. It starts with the attitude and energy with which you introduce yourself. Positive, authentic enthusiasm (not overdone) can put people at ease. They think that if you are so confident, maybe they can relax and feel like the solution they need is soon to be had.

Perhaps you can remember a time when you felt a lot more confident than you do now. A few setbacks or disappointments can erode one's confidence. However, you can reclaim confidence when you decide to do so. Remember what it feels like?

On the first day of school, Johnny's teacher asked everyone to share a story about the summer. "My dad took me fishing and we caught forty-seven catfish, and every one of them was forty-seven inches long," Johnny said. His teacher looked doubtful.

"Now, Johnny," she said, "are you sure about your catfish story?"

"Yes ma'am," he said. "Forty-seven catfish, and every one of them, forty-seven inches long."

The teacher thought for a moment before replying. "Now Johnny, if I told you that I was walking in the woods and a bear ran out and started attacking me, and a little Chihuahua came and killed the bear—would you believe me?"

Little Johnny replied instantly. "Yes, ma'am! That's my dog!"

I picture Johnny sitting up very straight, wearing a big smile as he answered so confidently it may have caused the doubters to doubt themselves. Confidence has a strong energy, doesn't it?

Here is something you can do right this minute: Check your voice mail greeting. This is often the very first impression you will make on someone, and first impressions carry weight. Why not utilize the opportunity? I won't coach you here on what to say, but here is how to record your greeting: Plan what you want to say. Stand up, march in place a few steps to get your energy up, smile broadly, and record your greeting. (Don't try to sound "enthused" at the risk of sounding inauthentic. Just follow my instructions, and speak naturally.)

When you are true to your passion, other people pick up on your good energy. Confidence, authenticity, and enthusiasm are like strong magnets for attracting customers.

Commitment Secret #4: Follow-up is Important. We have already discussed the importance of building trust—but trust is rarely gained after just one encounter. True relationships (business relationships included!) take time to develop. So, if you really want to motivate people to trust you and buy from you, be sure to follow up with them.

This is true even if they already decided to buy. What better way to show you care than to drop a note in the mail or to send an email? Keeping the dialogue going shows you care that they are happy with your product or service. It goes a long way in building their loyalty which translates into more business in the future, as well as referrals.

PERSISTENCE AND DISCIPLINE WILL HELP YOU ACCOMPLISH MORE THAN YOU THOUGHT WAS POSSIBLE — NEVER GIVE UP!

—DK

Relationships require persistent, consistent commitment. If you do not already consider yourself a "people person," you will be at a huge disadvantage until you remedy that. It is not uncommon, by the way, for a small business owner to not be great at communication and relationships.

Michael E. Gerber, best-selling author of *The E-Myth*, describes how "technician" type people, those who are really great at what they do, masterful with a set of skills that are being utilized by some employer, often decide to go into business for themselves. It can be a rude awakening for them to discover that being a small business owner requires an entirely different skill set and mindset, because relating well with others is a key factor in success. The good news is that relating well is a learnable skill.

Robert A. Rohm, Ph.D., is a well-known keynote speaker and world-class communicator. His keen insights into relationships, personal development, and personality types are invaluable to study and apply. I consider his material crucial in the day-to-day running of a business and as a foundation to attain Freedom to Succeed. Every business is a people business, so we need to do our best to understand people.

The initial DISC model comes from Dr. William Marston, a physiological psychologist, in a book titled *Emotions of Normal People*, published in 1928. He did not create an instrument from his theory, but Rohm did.

Rohm consolidated years of research into a practical approach to quickly determine how any particular person interacts with the people and world around them, i.e., their personality style. I found that the "Personality Profile Assessment" tool he developed produced a spot-on analysis of my own style of operating both at home and at work. It was an eye-opener! It gave me so much insight that I immediately thought of how it could help others, starting with my own staff. I became certified with the DISC model of human behavior.

The explanation I can share here about this brilliant tool pales in comparison to the experience of taking the personality test and reading the results. Nonetheless, I want to give you a sense of it. We all know that people exhibit different behavior and emotional traits, yet we are not taught how to incorporate that into our way of being. Think about the animal world. You know that you should approach different animals differently, and treat them differently. Based upon *what you know* about them, you would reach out to pet a dog who is wagging his tail, but turn and run from an alligator doing the same thing! The same holds true for the smartest and best way to treat another person—relate to them based on what you know about how they are "wired."

One thing I like about DISC is its simplicity. Rohm concludes there are only four basic categories of personalities, and after taking a written multiple-choice test, it is revealed whether you are predominantly a "D" or "I" or "S" or a "C."

Each of the four personality styles has its strengths and weaknesses. Strengths can be described as natural tendencies that are useful or helpful. Can you see how being clear on your own strengths and of those around you would be empowering?

In *Positive Personality Profiles* (one of Rohm's many published books), he writes: "When I finally began to learn these truths concerning personalities, I discovered (at long last) that God had made me a certain way. He gifted me and made me to be outgoing and people-oriented.....change would come as a by-product of His control [not mine]. I could actually *enjoy* being myself. What a freeing truth!"

Most of us have a basic understanding of human psychology. We know that people generally like to be rewarded, included, and respected. These motivations are common to humanity. Yet we also understand that people are different. Through DISC, we learn that everyone is most closely identified with the traits of one of four personality styles: "D" types are Drivers and Doers, and think in terms of "what?" while "I" stands for "Inspiring" and "Influencing" and will think in terms of "who?" The person who has dominant "S" traits is identifying with "Support" and "Stability" and thinks in terms of "how?" The "C" type person is all about "Correctness" and "Competence" and thinks in terms of "why?"

While it is fascinating to gain insight into what makes a person "tick" or how they are "wired," it is also helpful in a very practical way. I need to be aware of my "natural tendencies" when I work and talk with customers, vendors or my staff. I need to design an environment for myself that is conducive to bringing out my strengths. According to Dr. Rohm, "D" type personalities (I am a high "D") need an environment where there will be challenges to tackle. Also, "D" types work best when they have choice, control, and even some conflict.

An environment including these elements will help the "D" personality "rise to the occasion" and bring forth their best performance. Some of you may be thinking, "I would hate to work in an environment like that!" Exactly. You need to determine what type of environment would best suit your personality style and then do everything within your control to establish that climate.

Understanding yourself, your personality style, will help you to always work in harmony with yourself, not against yourself.

No one operates in isolation. The more interaction you have with other people, the more it is incumbent upon you to understand that people have different personality styles, and that relating to them accordingly is crucial.

Weaknesses may actually be strengths that have been pushed too far. Here is one example (but I want you to really study the entire DISC tool in order to make the best use of this information): When you are around an "I" type (because they are so people-oriented), you probably find yourself in a great mood, or at least more positive and optimistic than may be usual. They can be inspiring and contagious and often make excellent salespeople due to their power of persuasion. Now think of an "I" type person whom you have been around when their personality was out of balance and their strengths became their weaknesses.

Perhaps the "I" salesperson was so focused on having the customer like them personally that they missed an opportunity to close a sale for the company. In another example, the "I" type can underperform if they worry more about how everyone is getting along during the work day instead of whether or not the work gets done.

Potential and existing customers are not the only people you must learn to read, as in the example of the family business and the division of labor. As I emphasize throughout this book, relationships come into play at every turn of your business operations. An accounting firm came to me because of an employee retention problem. We all are aware of the investment required to hire, train, and manage a person critical to our operation, and of the cost involved in losing an established and good team member. I asked the CPA to make a list of things he had control over which could affect an employee's job satisfaction and commitment to stay on board.

Yes, sometimes an employee leaves for reasons out of our control—their spouse accepts a job in another state, or they have a sudden illness in their family which requires their time and attention, long-term. Focusing on what we *can* do to provide the best working environment is the key to reducing turnover and retaining good employees, I told the accounting firm owner.

Using the DISC assessment for everyone in the company armed him with priceless information to use in improving his company in terms of personnel and job satisfaction. One person later told him that she had been seriously contemplating leaving the firm before he made some changes based on the DISC reports. Why didn't she come forward before? Why didn't she make requests? What didn't she ask for that she needed? I told him that would be most uncommon.

It is your responsibility as the business owner and leader to ascertain what is needed and provide solutions, whether or not you get helpful input from employees. But with the DISC tool, you will have helpful input! The essence of the accounting firm employee's dissatisfaction stemmed from the fact she was an "S" type, surrounded and managed by other types who had no awareness of her style. She interpreted the lack of awareness as a lack of respect!

It turned out to be simple and cost-free for the owner to make adjustments which transformed this valuable employee's attitude and job satisfaction. In general, a "high S" person works best when there is an established work pattern in a consistent environment. They respond best to a leader who clearly defines goals and means of reaching them, and allows people to work at their own pace. Motivation is maintained through appreciation and giving the "S" a sense of security.

An all-too-common breakdown in business is the problem, chaos, and frustration that occur when a person is hired for a job which in no way suits his or her personality style. Also, this kind of mismatch often explains existing situations where a hard-working, loyal employee is so miserable that they quit just when you need them most. In the case of a family-owned and operated business, maybe they cannot quit but they can develop a bad attitude, underperform, and reap havoc on all the relations involved. I personally know of one example that nearly broke up a family and destroyed a business.

A certain garden shop in Tennessee was run as a family enterprise. In addition to the founder and his wife, two of the owner's sons were old enough to have many responsibilities, dictated of course by their father. I was brought in to help plan for growth, including how to expand their product line and hire additional staff. During a company meeting, I began describing and endorsing the use of the DISC program in the hiring process. When I spoke about how a "C" personality type tends to question everything, not to be disrespectful, but because they are driven to need explanations, I heard an unmistakable crying sound.

I turned to see the fourteen-year-old son with tears in his eyes, but now silent. I continued my overview of the "C" personality, saying that they are often moody because they are so task-oriented that having to interact with others is only an annoyance to them. The boy began to sob.

As his mother looked concerned and his father sat there, stunned, I asked the boy what was going on. As you might guess, he was overwhelmed by how accurately I was describing his own way of being. "You KNOW me," he said. He had seen himself in my description of the "C" personality style and suddenly felt what all human beings crave—he felt understood. It is always so validating when you find out that you are not flawed just because you are not the person others think you should be.

Not only did this pivotal moment lead to the implementation of DISC for the whole family and all new job candidates, it transformed the family dynamic. It was reported to me later that the sons were re-assigned jobs based on their strengths, and that their contribution to the company increased ten-fold. Communication drastically improved within the family, both at work and at home. This is how transformational it can be to learn the personality style of yourself and others.

Actually, everyone has traits of all four types, to a greater or lesser degree. The dominant one is, in my experience, crucial to recognize. In fact, you can learn the art and science of discerning others' personalities when you first meet them. There are behaviors that can clue you in as to their personality. No one is going to walk up to you with a badge that says "C TYPE" right?

In one case, I was handsomely rewarded for my ability to read and respect a potential buyer's personality type and treat them the way they wanted. The customer and his wife pulled up and parked in front of the large furniture showroom where I was a salesman. Because I was tuned in and actively trying to discern his personality type, I "knew" what to do just from observing the careful way he parked, discussed something with his wife before getting out of the car, and a few other clues. Standing twelve feet from the front entrance, I greeted the couple and said, "Good afternoon." He stiff-armed me and said they just wanted to look around. "When you're ready, raise your hand," I replied.

Then I walked to the other side of the store and discreetly watched for him to raise his arm. After one full hour of their self-guided tour and deliberations, the man raised his arm. Not only had they decided on the dining room set they wanted to purchase that day, he explained that they were moving into a new home and needed bedroom suites, living room furniture, and other items which totaled over $60,000.

With many other customers, I would have been in such deep conversation with them the whole time they were browsing that I would not only have known how many bedrooms they needed to furnish but the names and ages of each grandchild they expected as guests—and for which holidays. Obviously, buyers have different personality and buying styles, and relating to them with a well-matched selling style is ideal for both parties.

In the back of this book you will find the resource links to use for full understanding and coaching on how to utilize DISC, a terrific tool for the workplace, home, church groups, schools, and especially for salespeople and business leaders.

Chapter 5

Numbers Don't Lie...But Do They Fly?

Here's a big question I want you to ask yourself. If your business were in trouble, would you know it? If you're the captain, what if you are slightly off course? As a business workshop leader and coach to entrepreneurs, I have heard literally hundreds of people admit (or boast!) that they run their business by gut-intuition, for the most part. Even if your gut was discernible, being a little off course could be enough to send you miles away from your intended destination. That might not seem like a big deal until you factor in the tough things that can happen while you're off course.

What if a storm came in suddenly? Or you suddenly found yourself quickly running out of fuel, but were nowhere near the landing strip? In business and economic terms, you could be coasting along, thinking everything is great, but can you survive a sudden downturn in the economy? A slightly-off-course way of operating may not be discernible to the business owner who is checking their gut instead of their numbers. Staying the course is not only critical for captains of ships and planes, it is every business owner's responsibility.

This is a story about the day of my most important lesson during the time I was learning to fly.

It was a Saturday morning and it was storming. I was enjoying the luxury of a no-alarm clock day, sleeping in, and ignoring the thunder that occasionally woke me. Then the phone rang.

"Hey, David. Get yourself out here. We're going flying."

"Gary, are you kidding me?" My flight instructor, Gary, did sometimes have a strange sense of humor.

He told me no, he was not joking. "David, I'm going to save your life today," he said.

It was ingrained in me to listen to my teachers, especially the man who was helping me achieve my greatest dream, so I got out of bed, got dressed and headed to the small airport.

My car did not want to stay on the road, the wind was gusting so much. Pine needles and rain pelted my windshield. But when I finally got to the hangar, Gary was already there and the plane was ready to go.

The wind and rain had slacked considerably, and we ran out to the plane. I prepared for take-off, though the full, heavy cloud cover could not have been more than one thousand feet above the runway. It was not long before I could not see those clouds because we were part of them. Looking out of the small two-seater Cessna 152, I could not even see my wingtip.

We buckled our seatbelts even tighter, and continued to climb until Gary instructed me to level off, saying that we are at three thousand feet. The cloud cover remained a solid wall of white.

I gently steered the plane to the right, to counter what I felt was the plane's steady veer to the left. But the wind that was pushing us to the left did not let up, so I continued to correct to the right. All of a sudden, Gary, who had been silent, yelled at me above the roar of the plane's engine.

"Hey, David. Are you ready to die?"

My mind jumped to a context where that question would prompt my own statement of faith—so I said, "Yes." I meant, of course, that I was right with God, and would accept all things in His timing. I started to affirm that Jesus was my—he cut me off.

"Well, you're about to! Look at your instruments! We are inverted and going down!" Doesn't this sound like John F. Kennedy Jr.'s plane crash? I was about to die the same way he did!

As Gary's meaning started to hit me, I saw his arm in my view, pointing to the instrument panel of the plane. "Look!" Gary said again.

With my eyes now fixed on the instruments, I guided the plane to recover a safe and level flight path. We didn't die, after all.

By Gary letting me go as far into my mistake as possible without a disastrous outcome, he allowed me to experience a powerful lesson I have never forgotten. "Never rely on your gut feelings," he told me. "When you are flying, you must look at your indicators and go by the numbers."

Years later, that lesson came to me as a key to how to run my business. It was critical for me to figure out what my key indicators were and put in place "instruments" to inform me of what was ACTUALLY occurring in my business, rather than relying on what I FELT was happening.

I needed indicators to let me know if the business was up or down, drifting sideways or decelerating, or heading off course. In business-speak, that means I had to know my numbers.

Even if my business were only slightly off course, I realized that over time, it could end up miles from my desired destination. Many business owners, myself included, are not naturally numbers and accounting-minded. And we think there are more important things to pay attention to, like customer satisfaction, marketing, and high standards of service and product quality. While it is a good idea to frequently look up from your desk and take in the state of the business as a whole, if you are not regularly checking your numbers—your key indicators—you could be headed for a big crash.

A key performance indicator (KPI) is a business metric used to evaluate factors that are crucial to the success of an organization. KPIs differ per organization.

You want to always operate from your KFP (known financial position) and know your KPI's (key performance indicators). My instructor was right about another thing, too: he did save my life! So now, let me save the life of your business: know your numbers!

New or Review

You may already have your bookkeeping completely set up, and an accountant you trust to insure tax compliance. Having timely and accurate reports is one thing—understanding how to use them to make your business decisions is another.

It is so crucial to your success, and necessary for you to reach your *Freedom to Succeed* goals, that I will include here some basic terms and concepts that you can benefit from learning, or reviewing. It is not unusual for a business owner to have their accounting set up and someone to follow procedures, and then the owner (more or less) forgets about it. Not smart. Pay attention to your indicators! You need to know your "gross profit" just as much as a pilot needs to know their "altitude."

Why? Because that is the information which your trained brain can use to make your next move the right move.

As the leader, you face almost constant forks in the road where a decision has to be made. Have you ever wondered why sometimes it seems really difficult to make a decision? Maybe right now you can think of a decision you have been putting off. Whether of large or small consequence, do not make a habit of procrastinating when facing a decision. Often a decision becomes easy to make once you have more clarity, and getting more information and numbers at hand can give you the clarity and confidence you need to make quicker and better decisions.

Terms to Know and Use

CASH — Any type of monetary exchange (checks, cash, credit cards) is called "cash." Cash comes in from sources such as sales, investments, affiliate or referral commissions, or the sale of assets. Cash goes out to purchase an asset, for principal debt service, and to pay operational and direct expenses, including payroll.

The difference between the available cash at the beginning of an accounting period and that at the end of the period is called your CASH FLOW.

A financial report that reflects this is called a CASH FLOW STATEMENT.

Why is it so important you know about your cash? (I know you would rather have your eye on sales, right?) The reality is that businesses (small and large) go under all the time due to poor cash management.

For example, one ten-employee computer company in Atlanta, Georgia, celebrated when they were awarded a government contract to provide forty-two laptops and training to field agents. The computer company was able to purchase the equipment from their vendor on 30-day terms, a credit line they had worked hard to establish. They delivered the goods, invoiced the agency, and had a big fat number in "accounts receivable."

The company's cash, credit, and human resources were tied up in this sale. When the government still had not paid after 60 days, they were in serious CASH FLOW trouble. Payroll could not be met. Rent did not get paid. It was a nightmare. Do you imagine that a call to the government requesting prompt payment would have made any difference at that point? No, this breakdown should have, and could have, been avoided in the first place.

Being aware of and analytical about your KFP will help you make better decisions, including what projects to accept, which to pass on, and those that you can set appropriate conditions on *up front* so the numbers, and cash flow, work.

One more thing about CASH…that was the name of my cousin's calf he was given to raise. He was diligent in his duties of supplying the calf with water, milk and alfalfa. By being a consistent caregiver and responsible owner, my cousin ended up with something we all would LOVE to have: a CASH COW. Okay, a humorous name for a cow, granted, but maybe it will help you remember that when a business is said to be a "cash cow," it means that the cash flow is very much on the positive side. The company is flowing with cash like a dairy farm flows with milk. When you pay attention to your indicators of cash flow, your aim is to keep the flow streaming, never stopped. All aspects of your business will operate more smoothly if you have steady income and profit, i.e., positive cash flow.

INCOME STATEMENT — A financial document generated monthly and/or annually that reports the earnings of a company by stating all relevant revenues (or gross income) and expenses in order to calculate net income. It's also referred to as a PROFIT AND LOSS (P & L) statement.

Think about this: Robert bragged that his business did $400,000 in sales last year. Okay, Robert, except... that *means nothing*. This 400K number is an irrelevant number unless it is in context, related to other numbers.

Now, if Robert's P & L statement showed that his NET INCOME was 175K, up 22% from the prior year, and 10% in excess of his goal, he's allowed bragging rights.

Of course, every business and every industry has different ways to measure success when looking at their numbers. A restaurateur friend said that a *really* well-run restaurant can generate a 15% net profit; but even within that category, pizza places and establishments that sell liquor have much higher profits. Do you know what the average is in your industry? How do your numbers compare?

BALANCE SHEET — A financial statement that lists the assets, liabilities and equity of a company at a specific point in time and is used to calculate the net worth of a business. Total assets (what a business owns) must equal liabilities plus equity (how the assets are financed). In other words, the balance sheet must balance. Subtracting liabilities from assets shows the net worth of the business.

You may be the kind of business owner who thinks the above sounds like what accountants might excitedly discuss among themselves in their breakroom, not something you want to tune into. And that's okay. If your calling was to be an accountant, you wouldn't be putting your blood, sweat, and tears into your furniture store or other business.

Somehow, adding "net" in front of anything (or "gross" for that matter), always makes it more confusing. Simply think of your net worth as what you would have in hand if everyone who owed you money paid you, you paid all your debts, and you sold all your business assets.

Net worth is a tool that should be used when comparing your company to itself at a different point in time. It might be daunting to know the number, initially. But having blinders on will NOT help you win the race in the case of running a business. Get comfortable reading and understanding your BALANCE SHEET, and know the NET WORTH of your business. You'll make better decisions about operations and expansion. Also, you just may want to sell your company someday, and the net worth will be a big factor in that endeavor.

DEBT—Money owed to others who provided you a product, service, or loan. Most of us don't care for debt. We hear about the crushing effect of consumer debt on our economy. So why is debt for a business often a good thing?

The best strategy is to give careful consideration to your decision—don't automatically rule out borrowing money for your business, but certainly don't take on the liability of debt without due diligence. Personally, I have been fortunate (in my opinion) to start and grow my businesses without debt, and that is freeing. However, my advice is to examine your opportunities for growth. Give the business what the business needs. This is not the same as growing the business because it is what the owner wants.

If you are not looking at your numbers, you might find yourself justifying what you *want*, instead of making decisions based on what the company actually *needs*. Sure, it would be nice to have a new, larger office space. You think that adding another 300 square feet of technical support space would mean faster turnaround and more revenue. And you are positive you would be more productive if you had a window in your office. If you had a loading dock, it would save so much hassle and time. And time is money, right?

The decision to expand and potentially go into debt in order to acquire more space can be made way in advance by keeping your eye on all relevant KPIs. If the numbers tell you that your increased revenue and profits would pay back the debt (sooner than later) and allow your company to grow, then you can be confident in your decision to expand, even if it means you will need to borrow money to do so. (You will sleep better at night, even with debt hanging over you, if you know you came to your decision based on KPIs and sound projections, not just your whim.)

Some business owners are facile with using debt to their advantage. There are some reasons why a company should use debt to finance a large portion of its business.

First, the government encourages businesses to use debt by allowing them to deduct the interest on the debt from corporate income taxes. With the corporate tax rate at 35% (one of the highest in the world) that deduction is quite enticing. It is not uncommon for a company's cost of debt to be below five percent after considering the tax break associated with interest.

Second, debt is a much cheaper form of financing than equity. This is easy to see with a corporation with stockholders, but it can also apply to a small business. We have all heard about a business owner who takes on a business partner, giving or selling him part ownership in the business, in order to take the business to the next level. Too many times the partnership goes sour. Then the partner has to be bought out so the original owner regains 100% of the equity. This is tricky. Even when it works out, the cost to that owner was so much higher than if they had just borrowed some money at a good interest rate in the first place, instead of getting the money the business needed by taking on a partner.

These facts make debt a bargain.

So why not finance a business entirely with debt? Because all debt, or even 90% debt, would be too risky to those providing the financing. A business needs to balance the use of debt and equity to keep the average cost of capital at its minimum. We call that the weighed average cost of capital or WACC.

Remember, you don't have to be a Certified Public Accountant (CPA) to know how to count your chickens! The terms I am mentioning are measurable facets of your business that I urge you to get familiar and comfortable with. Your confidence as a great business decision-maker will grow.

There are a few other KPIs I will mention here that you have heard of—now ask yourself if you know what these numbers are today in your business, and how they factor into your budget and other decisions: Accounts Payable—money you owe to vendors, utility companies, or the landlord, for example. Accounts Receivable—money owed to you which has been invoiced but not yet paid by your customers. Balance Sheet—a financial statement that lists the assets, liabilities and equity of a company at a specific point in time.

Once you have all the basic reporting systems in place, you can add to your decision-making ability by tracking other measurable KPIs. Depending on your type of business, you can start by adding what you would find most useful. Examples include sales KPIs such as sales growth, opportunities, and product performance. In marketing, you may want to measure the results that a particular marketing campaign is generating compared to the cost of running it.

Also, whether you have customers walk in your door from the street or show up as visitors on your website, it is important to find out how they heard about you. Collecting and reviewing that data over time is immensely helpful when making advertising and marketing budget decisions.

A customer retention KPI measures your ability to keep and generate revenue from recurring customers over the long term. As you can see, the possibilities for different KPIs are many, but not infinite. Do not make the mistake of trying to track every little detail and spend hours poring over reports. Determine which KPIs help YOU make better decisions, and put systems in place to insure you have the numbers you need when you need them. These numbers are your indicators, your gauges to help you steer your business towards success.

Every business owner I know is good at problem-solving. You may or may not be the world's *fastest* problem solver, but you would not be where you are today if you did not have this as one of your strengths. This is fortunate, because every business I know has plenty of problems to solve! The great news is that the better you are armed with key information, the easier and faster every problem will get solved. Challenges that looked impossible, hurdles that looked like mountains, and territory that looked like a mine field will all become less formidable.

SOMETIMES WE WANT THE PROBLEM SOLVED, BUT WE DON'T WANT TO HAVE TO SOLVE THE PROBLEM.

—DK

Chapter 6

The Three "I's" of Leadership

We've spent a lot of time in this book discussing ways to make your job easier as an owner. Sooner or later all entrepreneurs realize that the freedom they crave has been eroded or consumed by their own creation—their business. Developing systems, as discussed in Chapter 3, is the best way to get out from under the tyranny of tasks and free yourself up to see the bigger picture. With a written systems manual, you won't have to waste your time training and retraining, or doing too many jobs yourself that are not the best use of your time and talent. Not only is this tiresome and frustrating for you, it can be disastrous—if you are tied up with working IN your business, who is left to work ON your business? How long can you stay on course with no one actually at the helm?

There are parts of running the business only you can do, and one of those responsibilities is the primary leadership. You are not only the owner of your business, but you are the leader—and being the leader is not something you can (easily) delegate to someone else. There are three components to leadership that you need to embrace:

- Innovation
- Inspiration
- Intentionality

A leader is an innovator. As the leader, it is up to you to break new ground, to decide when to try new products or strategies, and to come up with creative solutions when needed.

AS A LEADER, YOU WILL BE THE ONE TO TURN A WALL OF LIMITATION INTO A DOOR OF OPPORTUNITY.

—DK

Running a business may take "nine parts perspiration and one part inspiration" but at the end of the day, you are accountable for the inspiration part. It was your vision and passion that got the business off the ground, and you must remain connected with that enthusiasm to be a good leader. The word "inspire" is rooted in Latin—"God-breathed." People are drawn to and moved by an inspirational leader, many times in such a profound way that they perform and produce more than they ever thought possible, surprising themselves at their own capability.

Goals that require no extra effort are not worthy goals. To design a big game and then play hard to win takes a tremendous amount of desire. A great leader must supply the intentionality, the push for results, even when the going gets tough and even if everyone else feels like giving up. Different from inspiration, intentionality is about focus and determination. It's about bending a spoon with your sheer will when your business absolutely needs that and nothing else is lining up to make it happen. Just you and your intention.

Leadership Poor and Management Rich

As I was transitioning my focus from one company to another, I felt good about the state of operations in the company I had been leading, and had every reason to assume it would continue to thrive after I moved my office and attention to another business I was committed to building. I had put all the systems in place and worked through every problem. I had managed to attract some outstanding people and had spent over a year developing a great team of managers. I trusted the managers, the staff, and certainly my own systems.

For nearly twelve months everything was okay, and then I started hearing stories about attitude and relationships and people starting to quit. This person left, then that person left. I was surprised, since everything seemed fine and revenue was as projected. The money was in the bank but the smiles were long gone. I thought to myself, did I miss something? Are my systems flawed? Did I overestimate my managers' abilities to manage?

And then I realized that leadership and management are two different things. You can have all the systems in the world, and you can have great managers who diligently fan the flames to keep things going, but unless you have leadership, all will fizzle out. There must be leadership—inspiring and motivating people to become all that they were meant to be. Management alone does not cut it! The difference between leadership and management is that management does things right—leaders do the right things…like inspire, motivate, and encourage. So as you build systems into your company, please understand that you must have leadership along with great operations and management. Management comes from the brain; leadership comes from the heart. Both are crucial, as I found out when

I created a situation where one of my companies was, for a time, leadership poor and management rich.

Leadership vs. Management

You can hire managers to dole out the responsibilities, to teach and train, but leadership goes far deeper than that. As a leader, you have the ability to lead by example, to show empathy, empower, and engage not just employees, but your customers!

Unlike managing what already is in place, a leader causes something new to come into existence. To manage means to control or coordinate the operations and people, whereas to lead means to set and hold a vision for the business. As the leader, you are the one who sets the direction of the business. You also have the privilege and responsibility to articulate what matters, what everyone needs to treat as a priority.

At an early stage of business, you must meet the challenge of both management and leadership. As your business grows, it makes sense to hire managers and devote more effort to leadership. What you will eventually figure out is that you must develop leaders under you, people who can also inspire, initiate and provide enthusiastic intentionality.

Leadership and Ethics

In earlier times, business owners did not just plop down a new building or put up an "open for business" sign and consign themselves exclusively to their company's success. No, they were conscious of their reputation and were leaders in the community as well. They sponsored the local Little League teams, participated as part of the local government, were active in church and supported other community events. Sharing their business's prosperity, they donated money where it was needed most.

If you owned a business, you were looked up to. You would not be in business without the people (customers), and by showing up as fair, honest and caring, you earned their trust and respect. Acts of community support and leadership ensured that the business owner maintained an esteemed position. I believe this illustrates the biblical teaching (if I may paraphrase Luke) that more is demanded from those who are entrusted with much, and that with great power comes great responsibility.

DON'T TRY TO DO GREAT BIG THINGS AT THE BEGINNING

BEGIN BY DOING SMALL THINGS GREAT.

—DK

A business owner today can learn from this and hold him- or herself to a higher standard. Sure you can go through a checklist of ways to look good to your community or to pat your employees on the back, but what good is all of that if you have no real connection with anyone? Those that just go through the motions are not true leaders, but instead are pretenders. And pretenders cause a lot of damage inside organizations—and often in the community or entire marketplace.

How often do we see business owners in the news who were caught doing something illegal? They took advantage of their clients, customers, employees, and everyone around them to make a few extra dollars. They hurt everyone associated with the business. They became a disgrace to the whole community and were often chased out.

The foundation of leadership is integrity. No matter how big or small your business, no matter what corners you may have cut in the past, the first and highest priority RIGHT NOW is for you to take an honest look at the integrity of your business.

You must acknowledge your role in shaping organizational ethics and seize this opportunity to create a climate that can strengthen the relationships and reputation on which your success depends. Business owners who ignore ethics run the risk of personal and company liability in today's increasingly tough legal environment.

An integrity-based approach to ethics management combines a concern for the law with an emphasis on managerial responsibility for ethical behavior. As the leader of your organization, you must define the company's guiding values, aspirations, and patterns of thought and conduct. When integrated into the day-to-day operations, such strategies can help prevent damaging ethical lapses while tapping into powerful human impulses for moral thought and action.

A company with a huge integrity problem rarely has an evil dictator at the helm—it is more often the case that the normally-ethical business owner cracked under pressure. No matter the pressures, it is never a good idea to slip off the moral high ground, cut corners, or deceive your customers, employees...or yourself. It will come back to not only bite you, but to destroy your business.

In the 1980s, only two years after joining Beech-Nut Nutrition Corporation, the CEO found evidence suggesting that the apple juice concentrate, supplied by the company's vendors for use in Beech-Nut's "100% pure" apple juice, contained nothing more than sugar water and chemicals. The CEO could have destroyed the bogus inventory and withdrawn the juice from grocers' shelves, but he was under extraordinary pressure to turn the ailing company around. Eliminating the inventory would have killed any hope.

A number of people in the corporation, it turned out, had doubted the purity of the juice for several years before the CEO arrived. But the 25% price advantage offered by the supplier of the bogus concentrate allowed the operations head to meet cost-control goals.

If only an effective quality control system had been in place! An FDA investigation taught Beech-Nut the hard way. In 1987, the company pleaded guilty to selling adulterated and misbranded juice. Two years and two criminal trials later, the CEO pleaded guilty to ten counts of mislabeling. The total cost to the company—including fines, legal expenses, and lost sales—was an estimated $25 million.

Leadership in Action

Studies have shown that businesses that actually demonstrate *and* nurture leadership skills, creating leadership programs, often do much better than those who do not. No one is born with special leadership powers. Yes, they may carry themselves a certain way or be endowed with incredible charisma, but is that true leadership?

I don't believe so. True leadership is developed over time. It comes through personal struggle, overcoming challenges and setbacks, taking the time to reflect and grow as an individual. It is the ability to own up to mistakes and learn from them. Why is it a good idea to "forget the mistake but remember the lesson"? A mistake, by definition, is something in the past. Dwelling on it often has the negative effect of paralyzing action, and staying in action is a high-priority practice of every great leader.

As a leader, it is up to you to frame exactly how mistakes and failures will be handled in your company, demonstrate your approach, and teach and hold others accountable to follow your example. Believe me, you WANT to know when someone makes a mistake or fails to perform because only then can the situation be addressed and remedied. Have you ever had a tyrannical boss that everyone was afraid of? With no framework offered nor encouragement for people to own up to a mistake, you will be an uninformed and handicapped decision maker. That could cost you thousands of dollars and even the life of your business. You must establish the expectation that people come to you and let you know what is going on, even when the failure looks horrendous.

One way to help set the right frame of mind in your company is to talk about failure in terms of what it does and does not mean. It is important that your employees know you do not expect them to be perfect. Zig Ziglar said something to the effect of "anything worth doing is worth failing at."

Wow! You should let your people know that high achievement always means early failures. If you want to play it safe and never fail, stay in your living room. But if you want to play in the major leagues, you cannot throw the ball at your couch, hit it every time, and pat yourself on the back for never failing to hit your target. You have to be willing to be a beginner, and to fail time after time, until you can throw the perfect fast ball, right?

Even as an owner, you WILL make mistakes. When you take responsibility and then focus on what system component could be missing (vs. what's wrong), you will set an example and demonstrate how you expect everyone in the company to act when a mistake happens. This is leadership.

MISTAKES PROVIDE VALUABLE CLUES TO WHAT MAY BE MISSING.

A LEADER ALWAYS LEARNS FROM MISTAKES, MOVES FORWARD, AND DOES NOT STUMBLE OVER SOMETHING BEHIND HIM.

- DK

A true leader never stops learning about how to become a better leader. There's always room for growth, right?

Leadership Empowers Others

Another great aspect of being a leader is being able to recognize leadership in others. You can learn leadership through observation (again, a quality you want your employees to pick up). Do you have a set of role models, either inside or outside of the business? What have you learned, and what can you learn from them?

One way to gauge your current leadership ability is to look at how successful others are whom you lead. You can empower others to envision a bigger possibility for themselves. Your passion, commitment, and vision are contagious, so be sure you are fully expressing yourself.

You want to find yourself communicating (through both words and deeds) in a way that calls forth cooperation, alignment, and partnership of others.

The question remains, what's more important than improving your own leadership skills and how you are developing leadership within your business?

Leadership is Power

Oftentimes you will find someone "in charge" who is not playing the part of leader simply because they are uncomfortable with the power dynamic involved. It means there is a level of responsibility to leading others, including their livelihoods. If you give them responsibility and try to lead them, but they fail at their role, how does that make you look?

The reality is, you need to have the ability to make the tough decisions. There is no Systems Manual page with a pat procedure for leadership, but one of the regular tasks is making decisions which are in the best interest of the business. You will sometimes have to make decisions that are unpopular, that upset some people who disagree with your direction.

Before you know it, instead of having a nice group of co-founders and leaders, suddenly you have plenty of people who need managing. The heaviness of the weight of this kind of power does often break many leaders and can lead to a disaster in the organization itself. This is why so many shy away from becoming a leader and just try to manage.

Freedom to Succeed would not be complete without this emphasis on leadership. A common mistake that erodes the freedom of a business owner is when they get stuck in managing, and neglect leading.

What sets apart a good business owner and their ability to connect with customers is how well they lead. If you know your leadership skills are not the best, you can study and learn from the best! It starts with listening and growing. Find out ways to improve the lives of your employees and how to make your community a better place to live in. Start there and you'll never go wrong.

Chapter 7

Projecting Your Worth

I have a simple question for you. What are you worth? What is your worth to family, friends, your spouse, and customers? How valuable are you to your business?

In my opinion, you're only as valuable as you make yourself. I also believe that God values you a lot! In fact, you are so valuable to God that there is no amount of money that could buy you... you are priceless! If you think badly of yourself, I have some information for you: God did not create you to be mediocre, irresponsible, or ignorant.

There is greatness inside of you. There's a popular quote in church circles that goes, "God don't make no junk!" When I heard Zig Ziglar say this it really hit home. It is a great reminder that we are all children of God, though we often see ourselves as small players. How you see yourself is only a drop in the bucket compared to your real, true potential. Even if you do not have faith in God, you should know you have a purpose—it is up to you to articulate that purpose and create a plan that involves making people's lives better.

So how does this translate into the business world? A common mistake business owners make is to undervalue their main resource and asset, which is *time*. What does your average employee make per hour? Let's say $18 per hour. As an owner, surely you are worth more than that, right? How much more, though? Ask yourself this: if you had to hire someone to do your job(s), what would they expect, and what would you need to pay them?

Really, you are the center of the universe when it comes to your job. Think of all the planning, the sleepless nights, the blood, sweat, and tears. You handle the hiring, the firing, dealing with tons of stress, and implementing the plan and systems that makes it all run, day after day. You do ALL of that and so much more—so much, in fact, there hardly seems to be enough time to get it all done.

If money were no object, how much would you pay someone to do all the things you do? Here is an answer to what you *should* be taking home: a business owner is worth no less than $200 per hour! That's right—studies show that in order for an owner to do everything that you should be doing for your business, it is a minimum of a $200-per-hour job.

So why are you willing to do things in your business that you can pay someone $18.00 an hour to do? You could easily be doing the things that would bring a return of much more than the $200 per hour you are worth—things like systematizing your business, marketing, building strong relationships, building your team, and exploring new opportunities for growth.

Michael E. Gerber writes in his book, *The E-Myth*, "Work on your business, not in it." So when you are doing tasks, what is not getting done? What could you be doing that would bring a much bigger return for the company?

BUSINESS IS NOT JUST DOING DEALS;
BUSINESS IS HAVING GREAT
PRODUCTS, DOING GREAT
ENGINEERING, AND PROVIDING
TREMENDOUS SERVICE TO
CUSTOMERS.

FINALLY, BUSINESS IS A COBWEB
OF HUMAN RELATIONSHIPS.

—ROSS PEROT

The Power of Relationships

All of life is about relationships. Think about it—nothing in life comes about without a relationship attached to it somehow. This book is full of relationships! The couch you're sitting on is made because of a network of relationships. The coffee mug that you are drinking from was made through a series of relationships. You were born because of a relationship! All of life exists because of relationships.

So, if all of life is about relationships, and nothing comes about without the help of a relationship, then what is a relationship worth? Obviously, some are worth more than others, I will give you that. You? The person reading a book for business owners about freedom and success? Your connections with yourself and others are priceless. Your health, your state of mind, your relationships, and your time are much more valuable than you perceive. In terms of your business, you are worth at least $200 per hour. In terms of your close relationships, family and friends, you are irreplaceable and no price can be assigned to your immense worth.

Before I fully realized the power of relationships and the value of my time, I was in the trap of working *in* my business much, much more than *on* my business. The more I spent my time on service work, paper work, or doing the manual labor I could have paid someone $15 an hour to do, the less time I was out there brokering the big deals and improving my business relationships.

Once I started focusing more on building relationships, I started seeing evidence of the payoff and rewards this shift brings. You may be new and haven't negotiated a major deal yet, but let me tell you, the biggest contract I have negotiated for one of my businesses was $500,000. If I'm swinging around that kind of cheddar, it's safe to say I'm worth getting paid $200 per hour. But those kind of rewards come from investments. What do you need to invest? Time, effort, and intention to build relationships. Then you earn the big deals that keep your businesses flourishing.

Learn to Earn

Trust and mutually beneficial relationships never happen overnight. Do not make the common mistake of misguided expectations, like the metaphor of saying to the fireplace: you give me heat and I'll give you wood.

My parents own a jam and jelly business and had a goal to get into Whole Foods. I was excited to help them achieve that goal, and began to research what it might take. I soon found out that "Big Daddy" was the contact that I needed to win over, and let me tell you he was "Big Daddy." Not only was he a tall man, he had a big, larger-than-life personality—always extremely busy, stressed, and (of course) way too busy to talk to me.

So I went into relationship-building mode. I started sending him one email letter a month, doing my best to provide for him as much value as possible. I even sent him a sample pack of our naturally sweetened jams! I did this for 11 months and then he finally responded. He called me and said, "You're not going to quit are you? I love your tenacity and I know that I want to do business with you. When can we meet?"

Having a high-quality product was not enough. Having a very attractive label and package was not enough. Having the right profit margins for a wholesale buyer to be interested was not enough. The bottom line was, we got into 28 Whole Foods stores because of a relationship that I built. How much was that relationship worth? Quite a bit!

Imagine what you could accomplish with the relationships you already have if you would maximize each relationship to its full potential. I am reading a book right now by Bob Beaudine called *The Power of Who*. I recommend it highly. In this book, Beaudine talks about the power of relationships and that in order to accomplish what you want to accomplish, you do not need to meet someone new. "You already know everyone you need to know," he reminds us.

We just need to know more about who we already know. So think about who you know and who can help you accomplish your goals and dreams. Narrow it down to the top five and start building a meaningful deep relationship with them. Ask them what their dreams are, what you can do to help them reach their goals. You will see the value of relationships, and more importantly, you will see the value of yourself.

Zig Ziglar said it best when he said, "You can have everything you want in life, if you will help enough other people get what they want in life."

Can you make yourself more valuable? Absolutely! You are doing it right now by reading this book. Have you ever attended "Automobile University"? This is what Ziglar called listening to motivational and educational recordings while driving. Have you ever gone to a seminar? That makes you more valuable and adds value to yourself. The great thing about it is that when you become more valuable to others, your price goes up as well!

Now let's look at the potential lifetime value (PLV) of what a customer or client is worth.

How long has your longest customer been with you? I first learned about this formula from Howard Partridge, leadership expert and best-selling author.

The PLV of a Customer

☐ Average Job _____ X _____ (Average Annual Frequency)

☐ X _____ (Potential Lifetime) = $_____

☐ X _____ # of Potential Referrals Per Year = _____

☐ X _____ Their Potential Lifetime = $_____

Here is an example:

The PLV of Joe Customer

☐ $200.00 Average Job X 1 Time Per Year =$200.00

☐ X 20 (Potential Lifetime) = $4,000.00

☐ X 1 Referral Per Year = 20 Lifetime Referrals

☐ X 20 Years = $80,000.00

☐ (plus original $4,000.00 = $84,000.00!)

Plug your numbers in and I bet you will be amazed! Then pick up the phone and call all your customers and thank them for their relationship and that you appreciate them and their business.

All of life is about RELATIONSHIPS! Build, build, build!

Chapter 8

Sweet Dreams are Made of Goals

A high percentage of Americans, at one time or another, have considered owning their own business. A variety of reasons exists for why this is true. What about you? Think back to the first time you had a serious thought about working for yourself. Did you know right away you would do whatever it took to make that happen? To be the main person on top making all decisions AND the big bucks? It's a dream come true for millions of people.

Starting a business and operating a viable business are two completely different things. Sadly, most business ventures crash and burn before they even have the chance to reach full potential. In fact, Forbes reports that a whopping 8 in 10 entrepreneurs fail within the first 18 months. That's 80% of all attempts! While that is a staggering number of fails, it is possible to learn from the mistakes of others to help ensure your own personal success.

So why did those businesses fail? What differentiates between what works and what does not? The answer lies within your purpose for getting into business in the first place. Meaning. Goals. Drive. They all play a major part. Let me give you two examples of what I'm talking about:

Example One:

Let's say you work for a cleaning service. Every day you wake up early, put on that ugly uniform, and drink your weight in coffee just to stay motivated. And why should you be inspired? The pay sucks and your boss is a jerk. You are good at your job, one of the top employees in the company—but it doesn't matter too much, does it? Your boss regularly fails to offer any recognition of a job well done and, after a while, you get sick of it.

"Hey, I can run my own cleaning service!" you start to think. Not only can you out-clean everyone you work with, but you know the ins and outs of the business. It's time to take that next step. It won't be too difficult, right? There is no high start-up cost, no inventory to purchase, no fancy office with overhead required. All you have to do is find the right employees, train them, and pay attention to the details—and BAM, it will all work out! You're your OWN boss instead of slaving away to make all those profits to line the pockets of someone else. And what of your dream to become a veterinarian some day? Just forget it. That would take way too long.

Example Two:

Since you were little, you've dreamed of owning your own restaurant. Not just because you want to own a business, but it actually gives you great pleasure to imagine creating an establishment where people love to gather. You can see it in your mind: they pull up a chair and stay for hours, eating the food you've carefully prepared. As a child, you watched your uncle laughing and joking with his customers in his pizza place as if they were his dearest friends. Or perhaps you were inspired by your grandmother's recipes as she told a story about each dish, connecting them with your family heritage and her life in the old country. Food and relationships are connected and meaningful for you.

You also find meaning through volunteer work in your community, but you do not feel it is enough. You want to be able to be a much bigger contributor. Not only do you dream of having an establishment with highly satisfied and regular customers, you want to provide good jobs and training for people in your community. You want to play a big role in helping others reach their goals through your place of business.

You can predict the outcome of where each business ended up after three years. One ran out of fuel, so to speak, the other did not. I'm sure you see where I'm coming from in those two examples. The lesson here is that it is crucial that you follow your dream and your purpose! In my workshop for entrepreneurs, I stress that, "You were born unique to create unique things." It's absolutely true! If you feel you were born to run a cleaning service, that's terrific. More power to you. The point is not to belittle cleaning services (my wife and I own and operate a wonderful one!), but rather to examine why so many businesses do not make it.

What I am talking about is fulfillment. Joy. Passion. Here's a bold (yet true) statement: Many businesses started by employees and dissatisfied customers fail simply due to a lack of true vision and purpose. There was no dream.

The business you choose to start should be a reflection of YOU! Why? Because, in a way, it is you. It is your child. You brought it into existence. You did not just start a business because of a money grab, or because you thought you could do it better. No, you started a business because the idea and desire has been a part of your DNA your whole life. Thankfully, we live in a free country where opportunities for entrepreneurs abound.

The sky is the limit. Therefore, the idea and passion inside you can be expressed, manifested as your own company. The business is born and grows as an expression of your values, your interests, and your passion—therefore it is unique.

IF YOU WANT TO REACH A GOAL

YOU MUST SEE THE REACHING IN YOUR OWN MIND BEFORE YOU ACTUALLY ARRIVE AT YOUR GOAL.

—Zig Ziglar

My mentor and good friend, Howard Partridge, has a perspective I have learned to embrace: your business exists for one reason and one reason alone—to serve as a vehicle to your life goals. Ultimate success comes not by following someone's formula or ideas, but by creating your own. You're in charge here. You're the architect and have free reign to create your own vision!

But to develop that vision, first you need to dream.

Think about it like this: what reason do you have to buy a car? Well, it is simple. You want to go from Point A to Point B. You need to get around, to run your errands, to go wherever you need to go. That's it. It is a simple reason. But the actual type of car you get is driven by separate motivations. My first sales manager had me cut out a magazine photo of my dream car. He wanted me to pin that image on the board over my desk and phone as a constant reminder of my dream and my goal to make enough sales to achieve it. Goals are simply what you set to track the progress to your dream. Your dream is the final destination.

As a pilot, I always have the destination set of where I'm going (DREAM). Along the way, I set waypoints (GOALS) to track my progress and to make sure I get to where I am headed. If at any point I lose track of my goals, I very likely will not reach my destination. So goals are important to set if you want to fulfill your dream.

A DREAM WITHOUT A GOAL
IS LIKE A BIKE
WITHOUT A RIDER.

—DK

What is your dream? Is it a certain lifestyle? Extra time to spend with family? To travel the world? Solve a problem for thousands or millions or people? Enough money in the bank so that you will never have to worry about the bills again? Whatever your dream is in life, those dreams are yours. It is important to reflect, to check that your dreams are not actually the wishes or expectations of others. Your dream must emanate from within you. It needs to be crystal clear in *your* mind. See it. Believe it. Achieve it.

Leadership Breakdown

It is important to remember one thing: you're in charge. You have no one to fall back on when it comes to how you operate. This is your dream. It's your baby. And how you operate and relate with customers is essential to your success. Entrepreneurs who want to succeed will spend plenty of time improving themselves in personal development.

Here's what I mean: you're not only setting goals to achieve your dream, you are marketing yourself, in a way. Taking a major leap from worker to business owner before you are ready can be disastrous. That means your eyes are firmly on the dream, but you are not checking the personal goals you set yourself to ensure you are on the right track.

TIMING, PERSEVERANCE, AND TEN YEARS OF TRYING WILL EVENTUALLY MAKE YOU LOOK LIKE AN OVERNIGHT SUCCESS.

—Biz Stone, Twitter co-founder

It is quite amazing to see how many talented business owners there are with amazing ideas, but who fall apart due to their own dysfunction. We see it all the time with athletes. They may have all the talent in the world and even more potential, but they end up self-destructing and falling short of reaching their potential. Oftentimes, their failure is plastered all over the media for the world to see. It is a disaster of epic proportions, thanks to making poor decisions.

Since you are the leader and this is your offspring, you need to make sure you are someone who others can look up to. If you struggle relating with people, do what it takes to fix that. If you have anger problems, take some counseling or anger management. If your days and nights are spent on activities incongruent with your values and goals, it is only a matter of time before your business will implode. When you look for help, perhaps an influx of cash, know that there is not an investor on this planet who doesn't look at the personal character of the founder before pulling out the checkbook. Your reputation can either make or break you.

When you have finished reading this book you will be given the opportunity to evaluate where your business is well-prepared for success and where it is currently missing some of the puzzle pieces needed to complete your whole success dream image. The Business Diamond Assessment™ is designed to step you through ten checkpoints in six different areas of your operation: Procedures, Office/Tracking, Relationships, Leadership, Marketing and Sales. What you will discover (in addition to your strengths) are the specific areas warranting your attention and action. A leader's words are hollow without action. What I want for you is for you to leave this book IN ACTION, and with clarity of your most urgent and important issues to address. Nothing is more inspiring than being led by someone in action, with purpose, with focus.

Dream and Dream Well

School is back in session. Little Susie has just started kindergarten. It is the first day, so her teacher had all the children engage in an activity she knew they would enjoy. She gave each child paper and crayons and asked them to create a drawing of anything they wanted. She walked around the room, leaning over each child to check their efforts. She recognized a rendition of a cat, and of Spiderman. When she got to Susie, she said, "What is it you are starting to draw, there Susie?"

"Oh, Miss Stevens, I am drawing God."

"But, Susie—no one knows what God looks like…."

"They will in a minute!"

What an imagination, yes? Remember? Remember when you were little and your imagination ran wild? A big cardboard box was a pirate ship. A tree limb perch was a lookout for an Indian attack. A rag doll was a precious baby, cuddled and treated to a tea party.

Would you say your power of imagination was stronger when you were a child than it is now?

But you still have it….it may just be rusty and weak from lack of use.

Here is why you want to strengthen it and use it:

Einstein said, "Imagination is more important than knowledge. For knowledge is limited, whereas imagination embraces…" Well, what? All that is, and all that is not even in existence yet.

So, you have a dream. Maybe it's a huge dream that has never left your mind since the moment it was conceived. Maybe it was born recently, but the moment it was, you knew it was the very thing you wanted to do with the rest of your life. Is it something that is a family affair, or a singular vision?

Earlier in this chapter we took a look at how important it is to have a dream and goals that will keep you on track. But what is the ultimate outcome of that dream? What is your vision and purpose for wanting to go into business? Yes, you want to make money and gain financial freedom while doing what you love. But there's more to becoming successful than having a big dream and the right amount of passion.

By defining your dream, you begin to discover your purpose. Believe it or not, your purpose isn't all about you. It's about making a contribution to society as a whole. What problem or issue will you and your company solve? How will you improve people's lives? Let's face it. Unless you're meeting the immediate needs of other people, you won't do too well in business.

Earlier, in our Marketing chapter, I explained that there are only two reasons why people buy:

1) To avoid pain.

2) To fulfill a desire.

If you're not meeting one or both of those needs, your dream will never get off the ground. If you start a painting company, you're not just solving a paint problem. It's much deeper than that. What is it about you that stands apart from the hundred other paint companies in town? Why should the customer hire you instead of them?

The answer is: your uniqueness. Your fingerprint. Listen to the market and find out the biggest challenges your customers face. Then destroy those challenges. It's not about creating a basic fear so your customers keep returning to you for their slice of security. That business model is unsustainable and, quite frankly, unethical. It's also more than just wasting time or making a buck.

The BEST way to win customers is to stand out as THE unique solution to their needs. Don't make the common mistake of thinking you have to beat your competitors on price. If you went to the store to buy eggs and one carton was discounted because many of the eggs were cracked, would you choose that one and save some money, or the full-priced carton with a dozen perfect eggs? Being viewed as the company with all perfect eggs when a customer needs to prepare breakfast for their family is the position you are aiming for.

Imagine yourself walking along the shore while there are thousands of sand dollars on the beach. You cannot help but step on them, crunching them—they're everywhere. Your business may also be one among many in your town, or among millions in the global market. You know there are other companies in your field, and have come to accept that competition is to be expected in our free market society.

Actually, it's a good thing! Competition means a business owner cannot give terrible service or slack off on quality and remain in business. It means that customers have choices and that they do not have to settle for one-size-fits-all. To business owners, it means a wide open door of opportunity. It is a positive, not a negative thing to have competition. If I had worried about how many existing cleaning services were already established in my area, I probably would not have ventured to open mine.

Getting back to the beach, imagine that while sand dollars each are distinct (not clones), when there are thousands of them in view, they start to lose their uniqueness. It does not seem to make any difference which one you step on or over, because of how many there. But what if something bright and shiny among all the dark green sand dollars caught your eye? You, of course, would walk toward it, almost as if it were a powerful magnet and you had iron flakes in your shoes. As you get closer, you see that it is a gold-plated sand dollar! Eureka! Let me ask you a question: does your business shine like gold on the landscape of your marketplace? Is it unique? Attractive because it stands out from the crowd?

If you want to build a sustainable business model that survives even during tough economic climates, leverage how you are unique and provide a product or service that truly improves the lives of your customers. It will serve their needs directly, rather than creating other needs in the process.

Here's another interesting tidbit you might not know: customers don't always know what they want or need. When you really stop to think about it, how often do you realize you need or want something before it has been presented to you? For example, when presented with a new smartphone, you're rarely focused on what you need it to do. You don't think about the things it can't do yet. You just see what it can do that your previous phone couldn't and that's enough to meet your needs.

Think about the products we frequently use. The microwave. A lawnmower. When was the last time you sat down and thought about how these items could be improved? On the flip side of this, how often do we see a new gadget introduced on TV and we wonder why we didn't think of that sooner? It seems like such a simple (and yet practical) idea, designed to improve our lives, and often becomes a bestseller.

With all of this said, how do you go about defining your dream? Keeping in mind that this is your baby, remember that you get to design it. Anyone can own a business, but it takes a dream, a vision, and a purpose to build it into something amazing.

Steps to Defining Your Dream and Setting Goals (adapted from work of Zig Ziglar):

1) Define Your Dream.

What is your dream?

What is the vision of your company? Can you define its legacy?

What is the purpose of your company? What problem will it solve?

Ask yourself what it would take to create the perfect _____ company. How would it look? How would it operate?

2) List the Benefits of Reaching Your Goals. The professional, financial and personal rewards must be compelling or the slightest bump in the road can cause a detour away from your dream. WHY do you want to achieve your goals? This is where you get to think about your dream in action! What could be more exciting than finally seeing how everything will come to fruition? Let your imagination roam freely and write down all the good things you believe will happen. Once you actually write down these goals, you can have a better picture of what it takes to accomplish them. How will your life be "heaven" when you reach your goals?

3) Find the Obstacles. There will always be hazards and unexpected storms. No one goes into business thinking it will be all smooth sailing. So why not prepare and plan for every contingency? The best way to avoid the obstacles is to point them out beforehand.

You have heard the expression that "luck is where preparation meets opportunity." Setting yourself up for "good luck" starts with analyzing potential breakdowns and devising contingency plans. Do not make the mistake of not wanting to look for possible obstacles—be eager to find them and prepare for them.

When a train is coming at you, would you rather have your head buried in the sand or your hand on the lever that switches the tracks? Know where your levers are and when and how to use them if needed.

4) Skills or Knowledge Required to Reach a Goal. List what you need to know (learn to budget, better time management, public speaking skills, etc.) to accomplish the goal.

5) Identify Those Who Can Assist. Here's the truth: rarely will you ever find anyone who accomplished their dreams without the help of others. Make that "never." The greatest success stories in history had help from mentors and assistants along the way. Read books, attend seminars, and meet with other business pioneers.

As a mentor and coach to business owners, I am well aware that at times you can feel all alone with the challenge of operating your business, day in and day out. When you step out of the boiler room for a moment and reconnect with your dream, imagine yourself surrounded by people who want to help you achieve that dream.

YOU ALREADY KNOW EVERYONE YOU NEED TO KNOW.

—Bob Beaudine

One advantage of having a mentor is that he or she can point out what you don't know you don't know. Priceless!

YOU MUST LEARN FROM THE MISTAKES OF OTHERS.

YOU CANNOT POSSIBLY LIVE LONG ENOUGH TO MAKE THEM ALL YOURSELF.

—Sam Levenson

6) Develop a Plan. Your dream is the big goal, and, of course, there are milestone goals along the way. With each individual goal you have, it will be beneficial to create a blueprint on how you're going to reach it. Let's say your next goal is having enough capital to buy a local abandoned restaurant. How do you get from where you are today to having that money? Map it all out. Don't be intimidated! It may look daunting, but it does not have to be hard if you set your mind to breaking down each step and being smart about how to proceed.

By smart, I mean that you should keep the mindset that you CAN figure out how to get from where you are to where you want to go, and it does not have to be with a killer work schedule that throws you off balance in your health and home life.

Essentially, this step is bringing it all together so you have a plan in place. Right in front of you will be your defined dream, your individual goals, the deadlines you set to reach them, the obstacles mapped out beforehand, and where to look for help and resources.

Years ago, I learned an easy way to formulate a goal so that my chances of reaching it were significantly increased, and you may already use that "SMART" method, too. When setting a goal, be sure it is Specific, Measurable, Actionable, Realistic, and has a Timeline.

The step of integrating smart goals into an overall plan is important and should not be skipped, no matter how tempting it can be sometimes to let enthusiasm run wild and just fly by the seat of your pants, so to speak. Businesses that grow and thrive use planning. That being said, do not wait for the perfect plan, the one that is detailed and formatted beautifully with spreadsheet inserts, in order to get into action. The key is to START and then improve upon your plan as you go along. Many times, you cannot even know what all the steps are until you get into the game and find out. Then, you may use some processes that work, but don't work as well as they could. Designing and implementing systems must become part of your success plan (see Chapter 3).

A farmer I know had a small tract of land but an ambitious goal. To increase his crop yield, he decided to cultivate an area of his property that had been considered unusable because there was no irrigation to that section. He started hauling water to the area several times each day, using his truck. Not only did this get tiresome, he only did it during daylight, and for his purposes the area really needed to be watered every three-four hours, so he was not getting the results he wanted. One day he stopped his truck and got out.

He paused from working IN his business long enough to work ON his business, using his mind to think of possibilities and better approaches. It was not long before he got back into the truck and drove back to pick up some of his workers. He told them the task at hand was to dig a ditch. He had figured out a certain slope that he could use to direct water to the area in need. This is my "sell your truck and dig a ditch" story that I think illustrates that the best approach is often not the fastest or easiest way to operate INITIALLY, but once the system is in place—that is, the hard work has been done to dig the ditch—then everything just flows!

7) Set a Deadline. Starting a business takes a lot of determination. Having a lack of any true deadline to reach your goals can actually prevent you from reaching your destination. It can be scary setting deadlines, I get it. Not reaching your goals by the deadline can seem like failure, but you will have no true indicator of whether or not you are floundering or reaching your potential without them. Look at setting deadlines as a helpful practice to pull you along, not as if you are asking for stress and pressure. Setting a deadline helps you stay accountable to yourself and to everyone in your company and life who are counting on you.

"You do not have to be great to start...but you do have to start—to be great." We can all see the truth in this. Odds are, you won't go into this as *the* expert, but you can start small and begin to train your *Freedom to Succeed* muscle. No one wakes up one morning ready to run a marathon. Rather, they are determined to do so and train each and every day. Ziglar used the "block and mailbox" method when he decided he wanted to start running.

YOU DO NOT HAVE TO BE GOOD TO START.

BUT YOU DO HAVE TO START—TO BE GREAT.

— Joe Sabah

He set his goal to run around the block—said it nearly "did him in," but he finally did it. The next day, he circled the block and ran on past to the next mailbox. The next day he ran the block and two mailboxes. This is how you improve and grow, building upon what you've already accomplished and taking the next step. Before you know it, what almost "did you in" is a cakewalk.

This whole chapter can be summed up in a way comparable to a New Year's resolution. You have a desire to, let's say, lose 50 pounds. You know you need to lose the weight and you will look and feel amazing after you do. But it takes more than having just a dream, right? You have to not only go buy a gym membership, but you actually have to use it on a regular basis. Do you have the determination to see it through? To persevere to reach your goals?

Only those who keep at it, never giving up on their dreams and passions, will achieve great success. Please note: perseverance is a learned skill. Even if you have never followed through on anything before, you can learn how other people do it, and how to make it a strength of your own. By reading, studying, and embracing the two main points of this book, MINDSET and SYSTEMS, you will have all you need to succeed. You will, in fact, be Free to Succeed.

Have you ever heard of pluff mud? It is the locals' term for the dark grey, ultra-sticky and thick mud on the tidal flats in some parts of the southern East Coast. There are days when I feel like I am stuck in pluff mud. We all get stuck at some point! We notice we aren't moving forward, or that we're falling behind.

We look up and what do we see? The most gigantic, humongous elephant. That is, there is a problem, a confusing dilemma, or a difficult task which looms before us as one daunting, elephant-sized challenge. Here's what I then ask myself, and you can learn to ask yourself this, too: How do I eat an elephant? One bite at a time! With this mindset, suddenly I can just clearly see the next small action to take that will lift me out of the pluff mud and help me conquer the elephant. After that first bite, I no longer am focused on the whole elephant, just the next bite.

My dad's philosophy was that hard work makes good people—and he was determined to raise good people. Living on a farm, there was always work to be done, whether we were baling hay at one o'clock in the morning, or, at certain times of the year, working nonstop from early morning until late at night. Sure, I felt worn out at times, but it didn't kill me. Do you think we expect enough from our youth today? Do we give them enough responsibility and the training and encouragement to go along with it?

I remember driving my dad's tractor when I was seven, afraid I was going to put the thing into a ditch. The value of that experience has no price tag to me. Being trusted with an important job, an expensive piece of essential equipment, and encouraged to believe I could handle it were challenges/opportunities which taught me perseverance and confidence.

When you set your sights on learning something new, and have a strong motivation to reach your goal, remember to tell yourself: "If a seven year old can master a commercial farm tractor, I can do this!"

SET A HUGE AMAZING GOAL

THEN GROW INTO THE PERSON
WHO CAN ACHIEVE IT.

—DK

Living Your Dream

So you have this amazing dream and you know exactly what it is, or you know what steps to take to get the clarity you need and want. Once it is clearly defined, that's great! But keep dreaming. Perhaps I can say it best in a story I wrote a long time ago. It starts like this: Once upon a time a young man wanted to buy an island—it was a beautiful, lush piece of property. Although he had never actually been there, he would sit for hours and look across the bay at the island from the mainland. He would dream that someday he would own the island.

He had the dream and so he needed a plan. His was to build a bridge…no small task! To accomplish this, he set some goals. This part is very important.

His first goal was to set the first pillar. He focused on this project with 100% determination. You see, when you set a goal and implement the procedure, things will happen in your business. What is your first pillar, your first goal to achieve towards having your dream?

In my story, it was not long until the young man reached his first goal. Awesome! But, he still had a dream to catch and an island to reach. Now he must connect the mainland to the first pillar, which involves lots of hard work. To his credit, he has momentum on his side. He's on a roll! So he set another goal—putting in place the center pillar.

He's much further along than the other young men on the mainland who are still dreaming. He had a dream, put together a plan, set goals, and is reaching his goals!

When you set a goal the "why" is the DREAM—the island, a home, an airplane, or whatever your dream is. Your goals will be reached more easily, and sometimes seamlessly, if you work facing your dream. The young man purposed in his heart to never work with his back to the island. Keep it in front of you...never lose sight of your dream!

He is so focused on building his bridge that he doesn't even notice the remains of an unfinished bridge off to the side. In fact, there are dozens of unfinished, poorly planned bridges, now ruins, that were started and then abandoned. Maybe the reason was because the pillars (goals) were too far apart. Some of the bridges weren't even aimed at the island .... talk about not having clarity around your dream!

Soon he had the center pillar set and started connecting the first pillar to the second pillar. He was halfway to his DREAM! The island was getting closer. He could hear the birds, he could almost feel the sand between his toes and the hammock swaying in the breeze. You see, he never stopped DREAMING and always felt that his dream was close to being realized.

"Let's set the third and final pillar!" he called out to his team. You see, when you have a dream, a plan, and when you set goals and reach them, people and opportunities are attracted to you. People show up to help you. People like goal-setters and determined dreamers.

The young man started developing leaders on his team, which increased productivity. The project was going great! Everyone understood what the mission was. Everyone embraced the young man's vision, which meant that they loved building this bridge. This bridge was different... this man's bridge was going somewhere! The other bridges they had worked on were bridges to nowhere, but they didn't realize it until they got to the half-way point and then they gave up.

Over 50% of all businesses fail within the first year. Why do you think that is? Could it be that without a plan it has a greater chance of failing? Or is it the lack of a dream? Or not setting the proper goals? What if systems to promote teamwork are missing? Or could it be that there is no good way to gauge progress, so who knows whether the efforts should be maintained, doubled, or stopped?

How intimately do you know your numbers? Do you know how much it costs you to be in business per day? How much profit did your company bring in last month? Do you know?

MANY OF LIFE'S FAILURES ARE PEOPLE WHO DID NOT REALIZE

HOW CLOSE THEY WERE TO SUCCESS WHEN THEY GAVE UP.

— Thomas Edison

What happened to our dreamer? Finally, the day came when the bridge was complete. As the last form was laid, the last concrete poured, the final paint was applied, the young man stepped from the bridge to the island. He was filled with an emotion that only dream followers ever experience. Suddenly, all the hard work, all the planning, and all the team building seemed like nothing. It seemed as if it were yesterday that he started this journey. The journey of accomplishment, the journey of personal development, the journey of goal reaching.

The young man walked around the island and found it to be all that he ever imagined to be. Plenty of birds, flowers, and fruit...an untouched paradise!

He kept walking, living his DREAM!

As he kept walking, he came to an opening in the trail and could hear the waves coming onto the shore. Suddenly he found himself looking at the most tranquil scene he had ever seen. The water was a beautiful blue-green, the dolphins were jumping, and the sand was white. Coconuts were everywhere! But what really caught his attention, way off in the distance, was another island.

Dream Team, Dream Session

Surround yourself with dreamers. Put together a team that dreams together and wins together. The Bible says, "Where there is no vision the people perish." What would happen if you could inject a "dream virus" within your company that there is no cure for? Imagine your staff having the "dream virus" that allows them to dream about your company, and about their future within your company?

Imagine your people so engaged in your creation (company) that they actually contribute to the growth of your company. May I suggest a dream session with a dream team? Here is how it works: Once a month, ask your team, your staff, even your customers, "If we could create the perfect [your type] company, how would it look? How would it operate?" Let your team contribute. Let them dream. You will be surprised what will come from a dream session—this is a time that you want to listen, to observe, to take notes. There are never bad or wrong ideas in a dream session. (Teach everyone to avoid saying "no" and "that won't work" and to instead say "or.,.") You may not use or like every idea that comes from a session and you may not even implement the ones you like—but this is a time to let go and dream!

Not only can you hold dream sessions for your business, you can encourage everyone in your company to dream up their own goals. Have you ever wondered what your employees' dreams are? Shouldn't you know what these dreams are and how they can impact your business? The Ritz-Carlton knows what their employees' dreams are, and they work hard to make those dreams come true. Now you may be asking, what does a cleaning service (like my company) or any other "ordinary" business have in common with the Ritz-Carlton?

At first glance you might say very little. After all, the glitz and the glamour of a Ritz-Carlton hotel seems miles and miles away from the plain and functional maid service. But dig down into the Ritz-Carlton philosophy and you will discover lessons you can apply to almost any service industry, including maid services.

Ritz-Carlton has a culture where their employees are like their internal clients. They treat their employees like they treat clients with a policy called "…ladies and gentlemen serving ladies and gentlemen." They empower their staff and help them fulfill their dreams and reach their goals.

Imagine an "ordinary" company that takes an "extraordinary" interest in their employees' lives and the lives of their families! What does that look like? You may be surprised at how much an old-fashioned "company picnic" would be appreciated by your employees and their families. Did your assistant just return from a visit to see her mother who is ill? How about gifting her a pampering session at a local day spa? If one staff member is about to celebrate their 20th wedding anniversary, don't just pass around a card for everyone to sign—find out their dinner plans and send a limo to pick them up! What about cooking breakfast for your staff once a month? Do you know what goals and dreams your staff has? Are you helping them reach them?

Here's another important point: They're helping you reach yours—so take care of them!

Your job as a business leader is to make people's dreams come true!

Dream Test

1. Is my dream really *my* dream?
2. Do I clearly see my dream?
3. Am I depending on factors within my control to achieve my dream?
4. Does my dream compel and inspire me?
5. Do I have a strategy to reach my dream?
6. Have I included the people I need to realize my dream?
7. Am I willing to pay the price for my dream?
8. Am I moving closer to my dream?
9. Does working toward my dream bring satisfaction?
10. Does my dream benefit others?

I believe that if you really explore each question, tell the truth, and answer yes to all of them—the odds of your achieving your dream are very good.

Whether you say you *can* or you *cannot*, either way, you're right!

Recently, I was having coffee with a friend and in the course of the conversation he said, "He could never do that." I challenged him to consider the power of his own words. We need to be careful what we say, because words really do matter! Words really do carry weight.

If you remind yourself how motivated you are, and how much of an achiever you are, your mind will start to believe it. On the other hand, if you remind yourself how limited you are, and how insecure you are, your mind will believe that story. Your choice!

Say you can, and you will... say you can't, and you won't!

Chapter 9

Next Steps

From time to time, you will think that running a business is the hardest, most stressful endeavor of your life. You lie awake at night, worried about whether or not it will succeed. That is a lot of pressure to put on yourself. The thinking that got you into the position of being your own boss, especially your desire for independence, will not help you now. The key to success is understanding that you do *not* have to do it all by yourself. The answer for every successful executive, serious athlete, and motivated entrepreneur I know is having a coach. A coach is distinct from a mentor or consultant, and certainly different from a business investor or partner. All of those relationships can be important and useful, but only a coach has your growth, sense of freedom, and success as their only agenda.

We all need support and accountability. A coach will help you go from where you are now to where you want to go. I invest a lot of money on coaching, consulting and mentoring every year. I find it is *freeing* to have a structure of support that transforms my worries into wins.

Sometimes you need to ask yourself: To solve this problem I am facing right now, do I need coaching on my mindset or on a strategy? One self-coaching tip you can use is to keep your perspective of being able to hover above the fray by trusting the daily battles to employees, systems, and the momentum you worked so hard to generate. Don't spread yourself out too thin. Don't underestimate your value. And NEVER stop dreaming!

If this is what you've always wanted to do, you most likely have the passion needed to succeed. No one knows the industry like you do—encourage yourself to think creatively and focus on your strengths. Continue to look for ways to differentiate yourself and offer customers opportunities they will not have from competitors.

IT'S BEST TO BE YOURSELF.

BUT IT'S BETTER TO BE

YOUR *BEST* SELF.

—DK

Build relationships, as they make your job SO much easier. Relationships are key—you won't succeed without them!

Keeping your numbers current and making an appointment with yourself to review them regularly is one of your greatest responsibilities. Numbers tell truths you must be aware of—do not avoid, neglect or ignore them.

Continue to explore different avenues that will help you make more money, whether it's moving operations online or investing in new technology. Your Systems Manual should reflect a path of smali, continuous improvements, with frequent updates for streamlining procedures and being more efficient.

There's no way you survive without systems in place that run the whole show.

You can't grow your business without growing your people. The best way to accelerate that is to use the DISC model of human behavior. As you begin to master the distinctions of personalities and how to effectively interact with each type of person, your leadership skills will improve dramatically. Commit to understand and listen to those around you, and you will not only get to do what you love, but you'll also change people's lives. You will empower others to succeed as you succeed. There's nothing more fulfilling than that.

TO BE A LIFE CHANGER IN SOMEONE'S LIFE

IS A LIFE CHANGER FOR YOU?

—DK

Throughout this book I have urged you to examine every aspect of your business, whether you are a start-up or have been operating for decades. Never get too distracted, complacent, or fearful to look at your key indicators. This one mindful practice is so crucial to you gaining the *Freedom to Succeed* that I created a simple-to-use tool to help you get started. In the back of this book you will find The Business Diamond Assessment™. By answering a few specific questions you will be able to rate your business in all the key areas: Procedures, Office/Tracking, Relationships, Leadership, Marketing and Sales.

RESOURCES AND HELPFUL LINKS

www.EDGEpeergroups.com.com
— Master Business Coaching in a peer group setting

www.EmpoweringSmallBiz.com

www.facebook.com/DaveKauffmansystemscoach/

Dave Kauffman Presents:

1. Goal Setting & Achievement
2. Building A Better You
3. Building Meaningful Relationships
4. Leadership Simplified
5. DISC Personality/Communication Training
6. Five Keys To Balanced Success (KEYNOTE)
7. Marketing For Small Businesses
8. Turn Around Your Business With The Business Diamond Assessment™ Tool
   ...and much more!

Recommended Reading:

Think and Be Phenomenal by Howard Partridge
The E-Myth Revisited by Michael E. Gerber
Born To Win: Find Your Success by Zig Ziglar and Tom Ziglar
Raving Fans by Ken Blanchard and Sheldon Bowles
The One Thing by Keller and Papasan
Positive Personality Profiles by Dr. Robert Rohm

ABOUT THE AUTHOR

Dave Kauffman was born on a large farm in rural Georgia in an Amish-Mennonite community. It was there that Dave discovered he had the DNA of an entrepreneur. Not one to simply set up a lemonade stand, Dave decided he would go the extra mile and enlist his sister to help him market to the community and serve customers. Their customers ranged from thirsty farmers to total strangers. It was there that Dave learned about adding value, so he and his sister started baking cookies to go along with the lemonade. At six years old, Dave was running a profitable business, employing a person in need of a job, and serving new and repeat customers who were happy to get just what they needed from the two personable youngsters.

A little older and more seasoned as a business owner, Dave and his cousin started Best Team Auction Company, Dave's second successful enterprise—and he was not yet a teenager! In August of 2012, he fulfilled a lifelong dream and became a licensed auctioneer. He later went on and tried his skills at raising pigs and cows—it was through this experience he discovered he was not a farmer—indeed, his passion has always been in starting and growing businesses.

Today he owns multiple companies, all of which are debt-free and profitable. He is a pilot, scuba diver and an inventor. He travels around America and internationally as a speaker, business consultant and success coach to entrepreneurs. Dave is a Radio Talk Show personality, hosting "The Empowering Small Business" show on WSRQ (Sarasota, Florida) each week.

To gain the highest level of mastery in business and life success principles, especially those taught by the world-renowed author and speaker, Zig Ziglar, Dave Kaufmann became a Zig Ziglar Certified Trainer, Speaker and Coach. He also is an expert on human behavior, certified in the DISC Personality Profile methodology of Dr. Robert Rohm. Dave's education also has been significantly enriched by Howard Partridge, best-selling author and international speaker.

Empowering Small Business is the rapidly expanding company that Dave is growing to help businesses owners across the country by empowering their dreams of truly owning their business instead of *being owned by* the business.

Dave's wife, Toni, is his life, business, and spiritual partner. They are very active in their church and in mission work in Honduras and other countries. They live in Sarasota, Florida.

APPENDIX I

THE BUSINESS DIAMOND ASSESSMENT™

As I was working with business owners as their coach, over and over again I was asked: "Why do I feel constantly overwhelmed? Why am I still struggling to find freedom after years of working hard and seeing more blood, sweat and tears than joy and satisfaction?"

Business owners should be FREE! They should be happy and have the freedom to do what they want when they want to... and I found over and over that was not the case. I created the Business Diamond Assessment™ for the sole purpose of helping an owner like you find freedom in your business by following a course that begins with knowing where you are.

What is Missing vs. What is Wrong: This tool can be daunting if you approach it with apprehension, afraid you are going to get a poor grade in one or more subjects. But this is not a report card proclaiming how your business is operating right or wrong...this is to discover and bring into your awareness what is missing. You can always add a missing piece of the puzzle once you realize what is needed, yes?

You also will discover where your strengths lie. My coaching programs empower business owners to acknowledge and leverage their many strengths, discover what is missing to have a complete "diamond quality" company, and integrate the best solutions without delay.

On the following pages, read each statement and consider if it is true for you and your business today. In front of each statement, note your rating on a scale of 1 to 10: 1=not in existence. 10=completely handled.

Add your rating numbers to get a total score in each of the six areas: Procedures, Office/Tracking, Relationships, Leadership, Marketing, and Sales. Divide your total by ten, then mark the Business Diamond diagram with your ratings. Review your assessment. Which areas have the highest score? The lowest? More information can be found on www.EdgePeerGroups.com.

(1) MARKETING

Rate 1-10

___ I know the company's position in the marketplace and our unique strengths.

___ Our referral program consistently brings in new customers and sales.

___ We know the source of every lead and prospective customer.

___ Our system tells us the revenue results from every advertising dollar and campaign.

___ I have a Marketing Plan which includes a breakdown of coordinated actions, each with a schedule and person(s) accountable.

___ My website is professional, error-free and user-friendly.

___ My website and all on-line marketing is SEO (search-engine-optimized).

___ We have at least one social media marketing platform working in our marketing system.

___ We use our CRM (Customer Relationship Management) along with email to stay connected with our target market and customers.

___ We market to existing customers and track revenue from repeat business.

___Total divided by 10= ___
(put in the MARKETING section of the Business Diamond™)

(2) SALES

Rate 1-10

___ The sales conversation is consistent and professional, using a clear and concise sales script.

___ Each team member accountable for sales has written goals and a system for tracking results.

___ Sales pending and closed are tracked and reported daily.

___ Incoming calls are answered immediately and professionally by a person or auto attendant.

___ Inquiries and leads from our website are responded to personally within two hours.

___ Sales commissions and bonuses are competitive, insuring our company attracts and retains the best people.

___ On-going training is part of our sales department system.

___ We track results from a consistent effort to up-sell and down-sell our products and services.

___ Sales efforts are market-driven; we monitor and identify changes and trends in our target customer base, revising the script and approach to reflect our commitment to stay responsive to customer needs.

___ My sales team has the hardware, software and technology tools they need for their optimal performance and consistency across all sales centers.

___Total divided by 10= ___

(put in the SALES section of the Business Diamond™)

(3) PROCEDURES

Rate 1-10

___ All company policies are in writing and every employee has a copy.

___ Everyone is clear on the manner, prompt time-frame and method to handle customer issues.

___ We have automated computer back-up systems in place and have security and firewall protection for all our data.

___ Everyone knows exactly what they are accountable for and every job has one or more persons identified as accountable.

___ Records management is consistent. Retention schedules are in place and adhered to, including requirements for tax and legal file archives and disposal.

___ Our ordering system for inventory and supplies insures we never overpay.

___ Our Systems Manual contains the written procedure for every system in the business and is updated as needed and reviewed quarterly.

___ There are specific ways we set ourselves apart from competitors and these procedures are followed every day.

___ Everything that needs to be measured is measured, reported and reviewed regularly.

___ All 6 Business Diamond areas are reviewed every quarter to improve or streamline.

___ Total divided by 10= ___

(put in the PROCEDURES section of the Business Diamond™)

(4) OFFICE/TRACKING

Rate 1-10

____ I receive a daily sales report and review with staff.
____ I have written company sales goals and share these with staff.
____ Each sales rep has written goals which are tracked.
____ I receive a report on sales activity including closing percentage.
____ My accounts receivable and accounts payable are updated daily.
____ With my budget and tax plan in place, there are no surprises.
____ I review profit and loss reports weekly and monthly.
____ My balance sheet is updated weekly and I review it weekly and monthly.
____ Inventory reports including shrinkage and returns are updated monthly.
____ I have a system in place to track the results of advertising and marketing efforts.

____Total divided by 10= ____

(put in OFFICE/TRACKING section of the Business Diamond™)

(5) RELATIONSHIPS

Rate 1-10

____ I am satisfied with the number of full staff meetings we have –not too many or too few.

____ My employees are aware of and feel appreciated for their value to the company and to me.

____ I utilize the DISC Personality Assessment and know each team member's style.

____ I know my DISC assessment results, hire complementary staff, and leverage my strengths.

____ I have systems in place for employees to give and receive feedback.

____ I consistently provide training and other assistance to encourage employees' growth.

____ We have a CRM (Client Relationship Management) system in place and the database is current.

____ My company has a customer appreciation program.

____ I provide ways for customers to interact with our company and I foster a dynamic relationship.

____ We are active in our community on a regular basis with outreach and other programs.

____ Total divided by 10= ____

(put in RELATIONSHIPS section of the Business Diamond™)

Business Diamond Assessment™ © 2016 David Kauffman

(6) LEADERSHIP

Rate 1-10

____ Every employee has a written copy of policies and systems related to their area of work.

____ Everyone has a written job description including specific accountabilities.

____ Operations guidelines for each department have been developed with manager input and are clear to everyone in each department.

____ Team meetings are held regularly and everyone is on time and everyone participates.

____ The organizational chart for the company is posted and reviewed annually or more often if the company is expanding or diversifying.

____ We have a mission statement and a clear one-sentence version that everyone knows.

____ Our pay scale, benefits and salaries are competitive and help us attract excellent people.

____ My business plan is reviewed quarterly.

____ My vision and goals are clear to me and are written down for frequent reference.

____ Recruiting and training systems are in place, working to insure I have the best team possible.

____Total divided by 10= ____

(put in the LEADERSHIP section of the Business Diamond™)

THE BUSINESS DIAMOND
ASSESSMENT TOOL

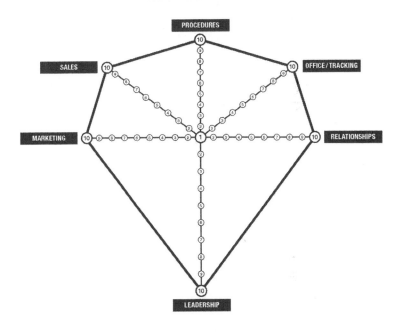

THE
BUSINESS DIAMOND
ASSESSMENT™

TOTAL SCORES

_____ Procedures _____ Office/Tracking _____ Relationships _____ Leadership _____ Marketing _____ Sales

Connect the dots on the diamond above using the total scores for each category from other side.

EMP**O**WERING
SMALL BUSINESS

Made in the USA
Middletown, DE
14 February 2017